101 Horsemanship & Equitation Patterns

A Western & English **RINGSIDE GUIDE** *for Practice & Show*

Cherry Hill

Illustrations by Richard Klimesh

STOREY
BOOKS

●

Also by Cherry Hill

The mission of Storey Communications is to serve our customers by publishing practical information that encourages personal independence in harmony with the environment.

Edited by Marie Salter
Cover design by Betty Kodela
Cover photographs by Richard Klimesh
Text design and production by Susan Bernier
Indexed by Susan Olason/Indexes & Knowledge Maps

Printed in Canada by Transcontinental Printing
10 9 8 7 6 5 4 3 2 1

Library of Congress Cataloging-in-Publication Data

Hill, Cherry, 1947–
    101 horsemanship and equitation patterns : a western & english ringside guide for practice
& show / Cherry Hill.
       p.   cm.
    Includes index.
    ISBN 1-58017-159-1
    1. Show riding.   2. Horse show patterns.   3. Horse shows — English performance classes.
4. Horse shows — Western division and classes.   I. Title.   II. Title: One hundred one horsemanship
and equitation patterns.
SF295.2.H55   1999
798.2'4—dc21
                                                                    98-55399
                                                                     CIP

Contents

WESTERN HORSEMANSHIP PATTERNS

ENGLISH EQUITATION 125

ENGLISH EQUITATION PATTERNS

APPENDIX. 241

INDEX 245

Acknowledgments

Thanks to Doug, Laurie, Rachel, and Tyler Krause, for being photo models.

On the cover, Laurie Krause is riding Fabulously Fancy, owned by Linda Collins. Rachel Krause is riding her own Bitasweet Conclusion.

Foreword

I am constantly amazed at how much information I must draw from in my teaching and instruction. I appreciate materials that add to my education and teaching. Cherry Hill's *101 Horsemanship & Equitation Patterns* definitely makes instructing easier.

Thank you, Cherry Hill, for the knowledge you share as horseman, coach, judge, and instructor. This collection of patterns, explanations, and tips provides valuable information and instruction for all riders. The guidelines are organized and easy to follow. Because the steps are carefully planned and visual aids are used, riders will have a better feel for their pattern work, which can only translate to improved organization and control in the ring.

Judges will also find the patterns in this book useful; they will undoubtedly inspire countless variations and new patterns.

A good horseman is a good horseman, whether performing Reining, Western Riding, Horsemanship, Equitation, or Dressage. All riders will benefit from this book, not only by developing better skills but by improving pattern work. Progressive levels of difficulty are offered to suit particular riders' needs.

To all who seek to be *better* riders, enjoy!

Carla Wennberg

Carla Wennberg is an American Quarter Horse Association World Champion rider and international AQHA and National Reining Horse Association judge. She has been an equine science program instructor for the last ten years. In addition, Carla has trained and coached amateur and youth riders in state and national competitions.

Introduction

Equitation is the art of riding. It requires correct overall rider position and effective use of the aids: the mind, the hands, legs, seat, and upper body. *Equitation* is generally the term associated with English riding, Hunt Seat, Saddle Seat, and Dressage. *Horsemanship* is the term generally used for Western Equitation, but it is also called Stock Seat Equitation.

In Equitation and Horsemanship classes, the performance of the rider is judged, not the conformation or training of the horse. However, an attractive, well-trained horse certainly helps to showcase a rider's skills.

Horsemanship and Equitation patterns are excellent practice for anyone who wants to test and improve their own riding skills. They are also very useful during lessons for both the instructor and the student to identify areas that require more work.

In a horse show, Horsemanship and Equitation patterns are used in conjunction with group rail work to evaluate youth and amateur Equitation riders. Each association has its own set of rules for Horsemanship and Equitation outlined in a rule book that is updated each year. (See Appendix for a list of associations.)

THE RIDER'S POSITION AND PERFORMANCE

Equitation and Horsemanship classes are designed to measure the ability of the rider to perform a set of maneuvers prescribed by the horse show judge. The judge looks for precision, smoothness, and balance. The rider should maintain a functional and correct body position yet remain relaxed and natural. The pattern should be performed with precision and a subtle use of aids and cues.

Regardless of height, weight, or shape, a rider should never try to force his or her body into an unnatural position. Each style of riding has its own ideal position, but in any class the rider should look natural. If, in the attempt to attain perfect posture, and despite lessons and exercises, you find that your ankle or knee turns out more than the ideal, learn to live with it and instead concentrate on the effective use of your natural aids.

THE NATURAL AIDS

The natural aids are the mind, the upper body, the base (seat, weight, and thighs), the lower legs, and the hands.

Your mind is your most important aid in Equitation and Horsemanship and, in fact, in any riding. It allows you to control an animal many times your size. Your mind provides you with the means to memorize a pattern, to visualize it before you ride, and to stay keen yet relaxed.

Your upper body assists you in maintaining equilibrium during the various direction, gait, and speed changes required. A mere tilt of the head can affect the overall balance of a horse-and-rider team.

The action of the hands on the reins is often overemphasized by novice riders but becomes subtler with advanced riders. Through the bridle, you have the power to influence the shape of a movement, the gait, the rhythm of a gait, the rate and length of stride, and the weight distribution between front and rear, and to slow down or stop movement altogether. You will hold your hands according to the head position of your horse and your style of riding.

Your base consists of your seat, back, thighs, and overall weight. The base is your connection to the horse and transmits signals to the horse's back that help to produce and control impulsion, bending, collection, and extension. Your base should always follow the movement of the horse. If your base falls ahead or is left behind, loss of balance and loss of communication result.

Your lower legs, acting on the horse's ribs, are the primary motivation for forward movement and engagement of the hindquarters. They are also the keys to lateral movements such as the turn on the forehand, turn on the hindquarters, and sidepass because the horse is taught to move away from the leg. The lower legs help to keep the horse tracking straight and also regulate the amount of bend in the horse's body when doing circular work.

Artificial aids are extensions of the natural aids and include such tack items as spurs and whips.

The Ideal Horse

The ideal Equitation or Horsemanship horse is a seasoned horse that is well trained and dependable. Stallions are usually not allowed in Horsemanship and Equitation classes. A mare can be brilliant but also unreliable on certain days of her heat cycle. A well-trained gelding is generally the most consistent, dependable choice.

A horse can boost or undermine your confidence. No matter how handsome or homely a horse looks, if he is calm, pleasant, and well trained he will make a good Horsemanship or Equitation horse. On the other hand, even if a horse is gorgeous and a brilliant mover, if he is excitable or grouchy, you will always be on edge waiting for him to come "unglued." If you are shopping for an Equitation or Horsemanship horse, choose a consistent and honest performer. A horse should be in good condition and show overall health and fitness. He should be alert, willing, and prompt in his response.

Class Routine

The class routine refers to the way in which the class is run. Each association has its own guidelines, and each judge will use those guidelines in his or her own fashion. Class routines are about the same for both English Equitation and Western Horsemanship, so the following methods cover both.

Method A

All exhibitors enter the ring and line up side by side at one end of the arena. The exhibitor at the beginning of the lineup works the individual pattern and then either rejoins the lineup, starts a new lineup, or finds a place on the rail, as designated by the judge or ring steward. When all exhibitors have performed individual patterns, the exhibitors are worked as a group on the rail. (See Rail Work.)

Method B

A prescribed working order is determined in advance. Each exhibitor is called by number into the arena. The exhibitor enters through the ingate and works the pattern. Depending on the class size and the space required for the pattern, the exhibitor is then directed to line up in the arena, take a place on the rail, or leave the arena until all individual patterns have been completed. Rail work follows the pattern work.

Method C

All exhibitors are worked together as a group on the rail. The judge chooses a prescribed number of finalists, often 8 to 10. The rest of the riders are dismissed. Each finalist is then required to work the individual pattern.

RIDING PATTERNS

Typically judges are required to post written patterns at least 1 hour prior to the beginning of the class. Usually the patterns are posted at the beginning of the show day. In some shows, the patterns are described verbally to the exhibitors as a group by the judge or by the horse show announcer. It is generally more difficult to visualize and ride a pattern that is described verbally than one that is posted, so be forewarned: You'll need to pay close attention.

In any instance, an exhibitor usually is allowed to ask for clarification of any of the pattern's components before the individual works begin. Don't be shy about asking questions, especially if you might be the first to perform the pattern. As soon as you realize you have a question, tell the gate person and he

or she will relay your request to the ring steward. The ring steward might answer the question for you, pass the question to the judge and get the answer back to you, or, if time allows, arrange for you to speak to the judge directly. Judges want riders to do well. It is disappointing to a judge as well as to the exhibitor when a rider goes off pattern because of a misunderstanding of the pattern. If you are a judge who gets a lot of questions on your patterns or if riders often go off pattern, you should consider redesigning your patterns.

In most instances, patterns are designed to be ridden in about 30 seconds so that the show can stay on schedule. Most shows do not time the exhibitor, but some shows might specify a 30-second time limit for the exhibitor to complete the pattern.

Rail Work

Rail work refers to a group of riders working in the arena, along the rail at all three gaits. Some amount of rail work is usually required for most Horsemanship and Equitation classes. How much is usually up to the judge. Rail work might be performed before or after the pattern work. Either all riders or only the finalists as determined by pattern scores might be called back to perform group rail work.

The group will perform at least all three regular gaits (walk, trot, and canter for English Equitation and walk, jog, and lope for Western Horsemanship) in at least one direction. Judges might also call for an extended jog, an extended trot, or a hand gallop. If a back was not included in the pattern, the riders will be asked to back.

Often due to show size and time, the riders are worked in only one direction on the rail and then asked to line up for final placing. In some shows, the riders are required to work in both directions on the rail. A reverse is to be made away from the rail in most instances, but some shows allow the reverse to be made either way, toward or away from the rail. If the judge wants to see a back during rail work, he might stop all of the horses and ask for the back on the rail. Alternatively, he might bring all the horses to the center of the ring to line up and then either ask the exhibitors to back one at a time or all at the same time as a group.

Avoid These Pitfalls

- Never feel silly asking a question.
- Don't assume the first rider was on pattern and follow suit.
- Know your left from your right.
- Don't forget to breathe.

Preparation Prevents Problems

Take the time to prepare for your Horsemanship and Equitation classes so that you don't arrive to learn that your horse is not eligible or you have left an essential piece of tack at home.

Read all show information carefully. Sometimes a simple oversight can be the cause for your horse or you to be ineligible for competition. If membership in a particular organization is required, there may be a space on the prize list that allows you to join simultaneously with your entry. Some shows allow non-members to exhibit, providing they pay a nonmember's fee.

Be sure that your horse qualifies for the class you are considering. Is your horse's level of training adequate for

exhibition? Check breeding certificates, registration papers, and age restrictions to make sure that your horse fulfills class specifications.

Are you eligible? Make certain that you understand the terminology of the class descriptions, the cut-off points for age divisions, and any requirements regarding horse ownership. For example, if you are an adult wishing to enter your 4-year-old horse in a junior class, be sure that the term *junior* refers to the age of the horse, not the rider. If you will turn 12 during the show season this year and it is not clear which age division you should show in, get a written copy of the system that the organization uses in such a case. Some organizations require that to show a horse in a particular class, you (or, in some cases, a member of your immediate family) must own it.

If you and your horse are both ready and eligible, pick up a pen and begin! Remember that when you fill out and sign an entry form, you are stating that:

1. You and your horse are eligible to enter.

2. You will abide by the association and show rules.

3. You are paying for the judge's opinion and will accept all decisions as final.

4. You will hold the show or association harmless in the event of an accident or injury.

Preparing for a Pattern at Home

Practicing patterns? It's a good idea to practice a wide variety of patterns and portions of patterns at home. It is not a good idea to practice the same pattern over and over again because that will just teach your horse to anticipate.

You should practice a variety of maneuvers and circles of various shapes and sizes to prepare both you and your horse for what might be asked of you. You should ride some patterns at home with the idea of "schooling" your horse in the pattern and others with the intention of riding the pattern straight through as if you were in the show ring without any changes, repetitions, or delays.

When practicing a pattern for schooling, to prevent anticipation you might lope right through the cone at the end of many patterns where you normally stop and back. Or you might stop and *not* back, even though that is commonly required. Some horses immediately begin backing after a stop, which can be a hard habit to break unless you give them plenty of opportunities to stop and just stand; stop and then walk, trot, or lope; or stop and turn. Work on doing the simple things well rather than rushing through more advanced maneuvers in poor form. Ride your horse regularly to keep him fit.

When riding a pattern at home as if you were at a show:

★ Ride it straight through as written, hitting the marks and not stopping to school.

★ Arrange to have an audience watch you and evaluate your performance.

★ Dress in your show clothes (including chaps and gloves, hat and boots).

★ Tack your horse up in his show gear.

★ Ride in hot, cold, muddy, and rainy weather because often that is what you get at a show!

★ School with other horses in the arena. Some horses don't like to leave the lineup; others don't like to pass or be passed on the rail.

AT THE SHOW

From the moment you arrive on the grounds, a certain code of ethics, attitude of sportsmanship, and set of manners should govern your actions. Some rules are specifically stated, while others are left for you to define. Know what the rules are, as prescribed by the sponsoring organization, and abide by them. And always follow the Golden Rule when dealing with fellow exhibitors.

Arrive at a show with the idea of doing your very best and learning from the experience. That way you will emerge a winner no matter if you get a ribbon or not. If you enter a show with the sole goal of taking home the trophy, you may leave disappointed.

At the show, try not to monopolize facilities that are provided for the benefit of all exhibitors. Be organized so that time spent at the wash rack or in the warm-up ring is minimal and allows all exhibitors access to these common areas.

As soon as the pattern is posted, draw the pattern, including cones and any other markers. If you wish, you may add the location of the judge, the announcer's stand, or where Mom, boyfriend, or husband will be sitting, for example. This will give you reference points for the actual performance.

Consider purchasing a half dozen mini-cones at your sporting goods store. Take them to the show with you so you can set them up in a small version of the pattern and practice the pattern on foot.

If you are at a show that is using the same pattern for all the Horsemanship or Equitation classes, be sure to watch other exhibitors perform the pattern to lock it in your mind, and take note of where common trouble spots occur. Think of what aids you would use to prevent those problems. Be absolutely sure what is "on pattern" and what is "off pattern." Be certain you know if the cones are to be on your left or right side for each pattern maneuver. I think more can be accomplished by watching others ride or practicing in your mind than if you school right up until the time you go in. Consider these suggestions:

Look at the arena.

Close your eyes and visualize riding the pattern.

Draw the pattern from memory.

Close your eyes and ride the pattern several times in an imaginary arena to lock the succession of maneuvers in your mind's eye. This should give you a much better chance of knowing what comes next if a performance error causes temporary confusion.

Your mind and body will perform much better with a steady supply of oxygen. Several deep abdominal breaths, pushing outward with the diaphragm, help to calm nerves and may help prevent memory lapses.

If the pattern is not posted but is explained verbally by the judge during the class, you will have to rely on these same visualization techniques to imprint the pattern in your mind. You will have to listen carefully to the judge's instructions, which are usually repeated twice, taking note of where the judge indicates he or she will be standing and where cones will be located.

Getting Ready for Your Performance

About an hour or so before you are due in the show ring, you will need to add the finishing touches to you and your horse's appearance. Have your attire organized and laid out, but before you put on those good show clothes attend to your horse's final preparation.

Your horse should already be bathed, banded, and braided. Clean your horse's hooves, top and bottom. With a damp sponge, remove any dirt or manure stains that have appeared since your horse's bath. Check for straw or shavings in your horse's mane and tail.

Once your horse is groomed and tacked, have someone watch over him while you quickly change into your show clothes. Present yourself to a friend for inspection (full-length mirrors are rarely available on show grounds). Be sure your hair is neat and not lopsided if in a hair net or bun, your hat is on securely, and your number is clearly visible. If you have long hair, wear a hair net or braid, and be sure it does not cover your number.

Make a final check of your horse's tack, mount up, and head to the warm-up arena.

The Warm-up. Warming up a horse consists of a different routine for each horse. A "fresh" horse must be worked enough so that he doesn't want to play in the arena, but over-riding a "mellow" horse may take all the sparkle out of his performance. In most cases, begin by riding your horse in a long, stretched-out frame for 10 minutes or so.

Then I suggest you ride the pattern once in its entirety in the warm-up ring. Following the practice pattern, lightly brush up on any trouble spots such as transitions or turns. If you relentlessly drill the horse just before you go into the ring, when you are in the arena he might shut down, lock up, or just take a break. It's best to keep your warm-up as just a brief review. After all, your training should have taken place at home over a period of months. You don't want to leave your best pattern in the warm-up ring.

The warm-up ring is specifically provided for those who will shortly be riding in a class. It is not designed for an entire string of horses to receive their daily training sessions. Longeing, coaching lessons, and exercise riding should be done elsewhere on the grounds.

When in the warm-up area, be alert and use caution and common sense when you pass another horse and rider. If all horses are traveling in the same direction, give a horse on the rail a wide berth as you pass; better yet, make a circle to delay your passing or cross the arena to an open spot on the rail. Even if your horse needs extra work in one direction, be courteous and change your direction of travel with the rest of the group in the warm-up ring. If horses are traveling in both directions in the warm-up ring, they generally are to pass left shoulder to left shoulder.

Horses working at the fastest gait should have the rail, but often this is not what happens in a warm-up ring. It makes no sense for the horse that is cantering or loping to be forced to the middle of the ring, while those walking or jogging hug the rail. If you want to practice a sliding stop or a turn on the hindquarters in the warm-up ring, plan carefully around the other traffic.

Just before heading to the show ring, you should limber up your arms, stretch your back muscles, and relax your neck. Take several deep breaths. Visualize the pattern. Think of the parts of your performance that will go especially well and give your horse a kind word and a pat as you head to the ingate.

In the Ring. Be aware of the order of classes and arrive promptly at the ingate. Don't crowd the entrance, but be ready to go in as soon as the gate person begins checking in numbers. Assist him by calling out your number as you ride in. If you have a question for the gate person, be patient and courteous.

Although you can check reference points several times during the running of a pattern, glance with your eyes; don't turn your head every few strides to look at the judge or a marker. That is considered an unnecessary affectation — the effective rider watches where he or she is going.

During rail work, watch out for other exhibitors in the ring. When passing is necessary in the show ring, leave the rail several horse lengths behind the horse you are going to pass. Move adequately to the inside and then return to the rail, making sure not to cut off the horse you have just passed. Causing the horse behind you to break gait in order to avoid rear-ending your horse can cost you an Equitation or Horsemanship class. And such inconsiderate behavior will make other exhibitors feel unkindly toward you. Try to ride the full arena without cutting corners.

Pay attention to the announcer's instructions and the positions of the judge and the ring steward. Don't run over the judge!

Continue showing your horse until the class has been judged. During rail work, you are judged from the time you enter the arena until the class is placed. Some judges will have the entire group of competitors continue to work on the rail as the winners are being called to the center. Other judges bring all exhibitors to the center to line up, and the winners are then called out of the lineup.

Although you can relax somewhat once the results have been handed in, you should not lose control of your horse. As the placings are being called, keep an open mind even though you feel your ride deserved the blue ribbon instead of the out-gate. Remember, if you were concentrating on your riding, you did not have a chance to see other contestants' performances. You might have done an excellent job, but another exhibitor might have turned in a performance that was a half point better!

If you scurry out of the ring frowning, you might miss the opportunity to hear a helpful comment from a judge who may have liked your performance so well that he or she wants to help you improve with a useful piece of advice. Although judges often do not have time to talk with exhibitors, an effort is sometimes made to provide bits of advice to youth and amateur riders. This depends on the type and caliber of the show.

If you do not wish to exhibit in a class that you have already entered, you should notify the show secretary immediately of the scratch. If this is not attended to, valuable time is lost while the judge and the entire show wait for an exhibitor who is not coming. Often there is a 3-minute gate hold for late contestants. It does not take many of these to upset a show schedule.

Tack changes, too, can delay a show. If it is necessary to change attire, saddles, or horses between classes, be organized ahead of time so that you can make the change quickly.

In most cases, a judge's opinion is indisputable. If you have a question about a placing, you should first go to the exhibitor's representative or the show steward for clarification. Ninety-five percent of problems are cleared up by an explanation of rules that were misinterpreted by the exhibitor.

Problems

Disqualification can occur for many reasons and are handled in different ways according to the rules of the organization. (Refer to Appendix for list of organizations.) Some disqualifications occur at the paperwork stage, such as a horse without the proper registration certificate or proof of ownership. In such a case, the horse is not allowed to participate in the class. Other disqualifications occur when the horse enters the ring. Lame horses or riders who are abusive or who school their horses excessively in the show ring will be excused immediately. The horse may be wearing illegal tack. Some shows will have a steward to point out the infraction to the exhibitor, and the contestant will be asked to leave the ring. In other cases, the improper tack may not be discovered until the entire group is working on the rail. In such a case, the horse is allowed to work with the class but will not be placed. Still other disqualifications can occur after the class has been judged and placings awarded. If it is discovered that a horse has an illegal substance in his blood or that he has been treated in an illegal or inhumane way on the show grounds, his winnings may be revoked.

In some instances, the representative or steward may need to confer with the judge for a clarification, and, on a rare occasion, the judge will talk directly with the exhibitor. If an exhibitor wants to protest a judge's or a steward's ruling, he must formally file a complaint with the show management, usually within 12 hours. The procedures vary with each organization and usually are quite involved. Most complaints simply arise from a difference of opinion between the exhibitor and judge and of course that is understandable. There is only one winner in each class, and only one person goes home with the blue ribbon!

Pattern Errors and Problems

During the pattern work, errors are bound to occur. A rider's ability is not automatically discounted if the horse makes a mistake. How the rider reacts to the error and corrects the situation is more important. The judge will consider the following when you make an error:

★ Were you aware the error occurred?

★ Did you allow the horse to continue inaccurately?

★ How did you react to the error? With anger, embarrassment, or poise?

★ How quickly did you react?

★ Was the correction appropriate?

★ Was the situation fixed?

★ Did you know how to prevent the problem in the rest of the pattern?

★ Did you maintain composure?

Areas That Receive Penalties

If you get mixed up and perform maneuvers out of order, add maneuvers, forget a section of the pattern, knock over a cone, work on the wrong side of a cone, or ride the pattern in the wrong direction or shape, you are said to be "off pattern." In some cases, being off pattern could be a disqualification, and you will not place. In many instances, however, being off pattern earns a zero score, which still allows you to place. For example, if you are an excellent rider and show great form and use of the aids during rail work, but when performing you go off pattern you can still be placed eighth in a class with eight horses. The riders in sixth and seventh place might not be as good riders as you, but if they performed the pattern correctly they will place ahead of you.

In some rule books, going off pattern is neither a zero nor a disqualification, but the work is still penalized. Sometimes a rider does a beautiful job in a pattern but then forgets one maneuver. Most commonly, this is the back at the end of the pattern. This is considered off pattern in most situations. But in some instances, the rule book notes that this is "not cause for disqualification, but judged accordingly." Although it is not a disqualification, going off pattern will certainly weigh heavily against you because it demonstrates a lack of both experience and familiarity with maneuvers and patterns.

PROBABLE DISQUALIFICATIONS

A disqualified entry cannot place, even if it is the only entry in the class.

- Not wearing the correct number in a visible manner
- Willful abuse of the horse
- Excessive schooling or training
- Fall by horse or rider
- Illegal use of hands on the reins
- Use of prohibited equipment
- Lameness

SEVERE FAULTS

Severe faults do not usually mean a disqualification, but the exhibitor is substantially penalized.

- Touching the horse with the hand
- Grabbing the saddle horn or any other part of the saddle
- Cueing the horse with the end of the romal
- Spurring the horse in front of the shoulder
- Omission of maneuvers from the pattern
- Addition of maneuvers to the pattern
- Turning the wrong way
- Knocking over a cone
- Working on the wrong side of a cone
- Kicking at another horse, exhibitor, or the judge
- Severe disobedience or resistance such as rearing, bucking, or pawing

OTHER FAULTS

Some areas and specific errors in horse and rider turnout and form are considered minor or major faults depending on the situation.

General
- Sluggish pattern
- No forward energy
- No collection
- Poor rhythm
- Impure gaits

Horse
- Tucked up in flanks
- Ribs show
- Overly fat
- Sullen, dull, lethargic
- Emaciated, drawn, or overly tired
- Lame
- Poor grooming, conditioning, mane and tail trimming, or hoof care
- Resistance when cued or reined
- Hesitation when cued or reined

Tack
- Poorly fitted equipment
- Dirty tack and equipment

Rider
- Stiff, artificial, or unnatural position
- Loose, sloppy, dirty, or poorly fitted clothing
- Poorly fitted hat or loss of hat during performance
- Excessive staring at a judge

Rider's Seat
- Falling forward when stopping and losing seat
- Falling back on lope depart and losing seat

Upper Body
- Head crooked
- Head turns in exaggeratedly into a circle
- Shoulders crooked
- One shoulder lower
- Looks down to check lead or diagonal

Other Faults cont'd. on next page

Other Faults (cont'd.)

Arms and Hands
- Over-cueing with reins
- Jerking, roughly pulling, over neck reining
- Reins too long, too short, or uneven
- Arms held straight out in front with no bend

Legs
- Over-cueing with legs such as spurring, kicking
- Loose leg
- Knee off horse and toes pointed exaggeratedly out
- Toes pointed down
- Legs too far forward causing rider to brace on the cantle
- Legs too far back causing rider to perch on crotch
- Stirrups too short causing too much bend in the knee and heels come up
- Stirrups too long causing rider to not have weight on ball of foot

Pattern Performance
- Wrong lead
- Breaking gait
- Poor circles (oblong, flat-sided, too small, too big, too slow, too fast)
- Counter-flexing in circles
- Falling in on inside shoulder during circle work
- Rough stop, horse throws head up, mouth gapes
- Crooked stop, horse's hip swings to one side
- Pivoting on the outside hind during a turn on the hindquarters (haunches)
- Crossing behind with front leg during a turn on the hindquarters (haunches)
- Crossing behind with a hind leg during a turn on the forehand
- Failure to complete the entire turn on the hindquarters or forehand that is required (e.g., 360 degree)
- Failure of horse to stand still
- Rough transitions
- Failure to exhibit speed change when required
- Sluggish backing
- Crooked backing

Pattern Instructions

Each breed or performance association specifies what maneuvers can be included in a Horsemanship or Equitation pattern. Rule books are updated annually and class requirements and scoring systems vary between associations. Be sure you have a current copy of the rule book from your association. Since 4-H rule books vary from state to state, there are not any uniform 4-H Horsemanship and Equitation rules.

Many of the patterns in this book can be used for 4-H, the American Quarter Horse Association (AQHA), American Horse Shows Association (AHSA), and other horse shows. When a pattern is designed more specifically for a particular association, it is noted.

In this book, the large dark arrows indicate the starting point and the finishing point of each pattern. You will be judged on everything you do between those arrows. You can make a good impression on the judge if you are ready and waiting at the starting point when the horse that performed before you is just finishing up. That way, when the judge looks your way, you can begin.

Always notice on which side of the rider's path the cones are drawn and placed. If they are drawn on the right, they must be on your right side when you ride the pattern. If not, you will be off pattern.

The dotted lines in these patterns indicate walk, the dashed lines jog, and the solid lines lope. However, at your horse show, the pattern might be drawn in a completely different way, so be sure to read it carefully. Also, note the direction of the 90-, 180-, or 360-degree turns so you don't go off pattern.

In most of the patterns, I have included a judge to show you a possible place from which the judge might view your pattern. However, the judge might be standing right next to a cone, sitting in a judge's box, sitting in a chair along the rail, or in any number of other places.

Also, in some patterns, there are letter designations but no cones used in the arena. These "free-form" patterns require you to plan spacing carefully on your own. In addition, I've shown various class routines you are likely to encounter:

★ Come out of lineup, perform pattern, return to lineup.

★ Come out of lineup, perform pattern, start new lineup.

★ Come out of lineup, perform pattern, take rail position.

★ Enter arena individually, perform pattern, leave arena.

★ Enter arena individually, perform pattern, take rail position.

For each pattern, there are three sets of information. First, on the pattern itself, you will find the "bare-bones" pattern instructions as they would be written by a horse show judge and posted at a show. They are brief. Next, you will find Pattern Help, which provides you with aids and reminders as you ride each portion of the pattern. You will see references to other patterns that contain similar maneuvers and transitions. Finally, with each pattern, I have included a training or riding tip that is specific to that pattern but that is applicable to many other patterns as well.

I have grouped the patterns into Beginning, Intermediate, and Advanced sections. The patterns are listed in approximate order of difficulty within the groups. I suggest that you start with the beginning patterns even if you are an experienced rider. At the start of each section, you'll find four blank arenas where you can draw patterns you've ridden at shows.

Remember, it is better to do simple things well than to blunder through advanced maneuvers in poor form.

ARENA MAP KEY

cone	◎
imaginary point	●
start/end	⬅
walk	· · · · · · · · · · ·
trot/jog	— — — — — —
change of diagonal	— — ⁄ — —
canter/lope	————————
simple lead change through walk	——— · · ———
simple lead change through trot/jog	——— — — ———
flying lead change	——— 8 ———
stop/halt	|
back	→ → → → →
forehand/hindquarter turn	↻

Western Horsemanship

Western Horsemanship is also called Western Equitation or Stock Seat Equitation. It refers to a class that tests a rider's skills and communication with his or her horse. A somewhat confusing point is that horsemanship is also a general term used to describe effective English or Western riding, training, horse handling, and care in or out of the show ring.

What Is Good Horsemanship?

A Western Horsemanship rider must be relaxed and comfortable performing a set of prescribed maneuvers while mounted. Your performance should be precise and smooth, and you should exhibit poise and confidence while maintaining a balanced, functional, and fundamentally correct body position. Aids should be subtle, responses prompt. The best way to prepare for a good performance in the show arena is to spend plenty of hours practicing various maneuvers in a variety of arenas and locations.

Seat. Your position in the saddle should appear natural. Regardless of the maneuver or gait being performed, your position should be consistent. Your seat should be secure yet relaxed. You should sit in the center of the saddle, which should be positioned in the center of the horse's back. Your seat and inner thigh should maintain a close contact with the saddle. Your back should be flat, relaxed, and supple. An overly stiff or overly arched lower back is undesirable because it is less secure.

Upper Body. You should maintain an upright position with your upper body at all gaits. Your sternum should be forward, your shoulders back. A collapsed chest and shoulders that roll forward inhibit the free movement of a rider's arms and make the seat less secure. Shoulders should be level, not one lower than the other. They should also be square to the trunk of your body, not one leading the other. Your head should be held with your chin level and your eyes forward. Your head may be directed slightly toward the direction of travel, but excessive turning of your head to the inside of a circle or down at the horse's head or shoulder unbalances you and you can't see where you are going. This will be penalized.

Legs. Your legs should hang to form a straight line from your ear through the center of your shoulder and hip, and the line should either touch the back of your heel or bisect your ankle. Your stirrups should be just short enough to allow your heels to be lower than your toes, with a slight bend in your knees. Your lower legs should be directly under your knees. If you glance down, you shouldn't be able to see your feet. Your weight should be directly over the balls of your feet. If your horse were to suddenly disappear from underneath you, you should be standing! Light contact should be maintained with the saddle and the horse from your knees to midcalf in order to give aids to the horse. The "A-frame" position, where the legs are held exaggeratedly away from the horse's sides, is ineffective and will be penalized. Your knees should point forward and remain closed with no space between your knees and the saddle. You will be penalized for positioning your legs excessively behind or forward of the vertical position. Regardless of the type of stirrup you use, your feet may be placed "home" in the stirrup, with your boot heels touching the stirrups, or they may be placed with the balls of your feet in the center of the stirrup tread. Your toes should point straight ahead or slightly out with your ankles straight or very slightly broken in. Riding with only your toes in the stirrup is a weak position and will be penalized. If you can maintain proper position throughout all pattern and rail work, you will receive more credit.

Arms. Both hands and arms should be held in a relaxed, easy manner with the upper arm in a straight line with the body. The arm holding the reins should be bent at the elbow, forming a line from your elbow to the horse's mouth. The free hand and arm may be straight down at your side or carried bent at the elbow in a similar position as the hand holding the reins. Whichever method you choose, be sure it looks natural. Excessive pumping or flapping of your free arm or excessive stiffness will be penalized. The free hand should be kept away from the horse and equipment.

Bracing against the horn with either hand will be penalized. The wrist of your reining hand should be straight and relaxed with your hand rotated inward about 30 to 45 degrees inside the vertical. This forms a half roof over the withers. Your rein hand should be carried immediately above or slightly in front of the saddle horn. Only one hand is to be used for reining, and hands shall not be changed. The reining hand is to be around the reins; one finger between the reins is permissible.

Junior horses (5 years and under) shown with a bosal or snaffle bit may be ridden with two hands on the reins. When a curb bit is used, only one hand may be used on the reins, and the hand must not be changed. The hand is to be around the reins; index finger only between split reins is permitted. Violation of this rule is an automatic disqualification.

A romal is an extension of braided material attached to closed reins. The closed rein portion is held in the reining hand; no fingers are allowed between the closed reins. Your rule book will specify whether the romal may be carried in the free hand to keep it from swinging and to adjust rein length or if your free hand, holding the romal, should rest on your leg. There must be at least a 16-inch (40.6-cm) spacing between the reining hand and the free hand holding the romal.

The reins should be adjusted so that you have light contact with the horse's mouth. At no time should the reins require more than a slight hand movement to control the horse. Excessively tight or loose reins will be penalized.

Position in Motion. You should sit both the jog and the extended jog and not post. At the lope, you should be glued; that is, there shouldn't be "daylight" between your seat and the saddle. Your upper body should remain still and vertical. All movements of the horse should be governed by the use of imperceptible aids. Using exaggerated shifting of your weight as a cue is not desirable. When requested to ride without stirrups, you should maintain the same position as previously described. The stirrups dangle along the horse's side.

Areas that receive penalties and disqualification are discussed in the Introduction. In addition, the following rider errors are associated specifically with Western Horsemanship:

★ Grabbing the saddle horn

★ Cueing the horse with the end of the romal

★ Using more than one finger between split reins

- ★ Using any fingers between closed reins
- ★ Over-cueing with the neck rein
- ★ Bracing against the cantle
- ★ Pivoting on the outside hind during a turn on the hindquarters
- ★ Wearing a poorly fitting hat
- ★ Losing your hat during the performance

TACK

The horse must be shown in a western saddle. Horses 5 years old and younger may be shown in a snaffle bit, hackamore, curb bit, half-breed, or spade bit. Horses 6 years old and older may only be shown in a curb bit, half-breed, or spade bit. When a curb bit is used, a curb strap or curb chain is required and must meet the judge's approval. It must be at least ½ inch (1.3 cm) in width and lie flat against the jaw of the horse.

The saddle, bridle, and saddle blanket should fit the horse properly and be neat, clean, and in good repair.

Optional equipment often includes protective boots, leg wraps, bandages, and spurs.

Illegal Equipment

Chin straps narrower than ½ inch (1.3 cm), martingales, nosebands, tie downs, mechanical hackamores, and wire chin straps are all prohibited from the show ring.

GAITS

Gaits are the natural footfall sequences a horse performs. In order to be correct, a gait must have a clean, distinct rhythm as outlined in each definition.

Walk. The walk is a natural, flat-footed 4-beat gait where the horse moves straight with his hind feet following the lines of travel of his front feet. Flat-footed means the hoof lands flat, not toe or heel first, which would indicate that the horse is verging on a jog, jigging, or prancing. The horse's expression at the walk should be alert, with a reasonable length of stride in keeping with the size of the horse.

Jog. The western jog is a smooth 2-beat diagonal gait. The jog should be very even in rhythm from one diagonal pair of legs to the other. The horse should track straight with the hind feet following in the tracks of the front feet.

Extended Jog. The extended jog is an increase in stride length without an increase in rhythm. The legs don't move quicker, but the legs do reach farther, resulting in a longer, more ground-covering stride. The extended jog should be smooth.

Lope. The lope is an easy 3-beat gait that is rhythmical and smooth. When a horse is moving to the left, he should be on the left lead unless a counter-canter has been requested. When moving to the right, he should be on the right lead. If a horse is loping with 4 beats, the diagonal pair has broken and he is not performing a true gait. This will be penalized. In Horsemanship, a rider is expected to easily feel this error and correct it by moving the horse forward into a 3-beat lope.

Counter-Canter. A counter-canter is a deliberate lope on the lead opposite the direction in which the horse is traveling.

It is not a lope on the "wrong" lead. When a horse can be cued to lope on the lead opposite to the direction of travel, he is exhibiting great training, balance, and strength. It is a maneuver that shows whether a horse is just performing robotically or if the rider is effectively riding the horse. Even though canter is the term used to refer to the English gait that is most similar to the lope, even in Western riding the term *counter-canter* (rather than counter-lope) is used.

Extended Lope. The extended lope is an increase in stride length without an increase in rhythm. The legs don't move quicker, but they do reach farther, resulting in a longer, more ground-covering stride.

Gallop. The gallop has a longer stride and faster rhythm than the lope or the extended lope. The gallop is more often used in reining classes but is sometimes called for in Horsemanship as well.

Back. The back is a 2-beat diagonal gait in reverse. A back will usually be asked for in the individual pattern; if not, it will be asked for in the group rail work. Your horse should back on a loose rein with his neck low and round. As he backs, his croup should lower, his hind legs should be well under his belly, and he should flex his abdominals. All this will help him move his legs backward most efficiently. He should not shuffle or drag his feet backward; he should step crisply and distinctly. When a horse throws his head up or stiffens his back, his body locks up. This shows that his training and that of the rider need work.

Maneuvers

Maneuvers are changes in direction, speed, or length of stride. Turns are often called for following a stop, but maneuvers can be incorporated into patterns in a variety of ways. Maneuvers test a rider's control and precision in the application of all aids.

Straight Lines. On the straight lines of a pattern, the horse should track straight. His head and neck should be straight in line with his body. His hind feet should follow the tracks of his front feet. The horse's body should not be at an angle. This error is especially evident at the lope.

Curved Lines. The horse's head and neck should be slightly bent to the inside on arcing lines and circles. His body should bend in a uniform curve with his hind feet following the tracks of his front feet.

Serpentine. A serpentine is a snakelike pattern that can be a shallow wave or a series of half circles connected by straight lines.

Circle. A circle should be evenly round and the two halves of the circle should be equal in size. Circles should be performed at the appropriate speed, size, and location as indicated by the pattern.

Figure 8. A figure 8 consists of two circles that touch at one point resulting in a figure that looks like the number eight.

Stop. A stop should be straight, square, prompt, smooth, and the horse's body should remain straight during the entire maneuver. The horse's back should round slightly, not hollow, during a stop. His head position should remain relatively consistent. A stop is the Western term for a halt.

Turn. Turns should be smooth and have a continuous flow, not jerkiness, to them. Western horses should neck rein from the lightest touch.

Pivot. A pivot is a 90-degree turn on the hindquarters from a standstill.

Spin. A spin, also called a turnaround, is a reining maneuver that is a turn on the hindquarters at speed. Since a spin relates more to specialized training of a horse for reining, I have not included any spins in the patterns in this book. However, because they are listed as potential inclusions in several rule books, you need to know about the possibility of their appearance.

Rollback. A rollback is a lope and a set (brief stop) and a 180-degree turn over the hocks without hesitation or loss of momentum. The horse does not come to a full stop between the lope and the turn. Backing during the turn would be penalized. Usually a horse lopes into and out of a rollback. A rollback is a specialized reining maneuver not often required in Horsemanship.

Turn on the Forehand. When performing a turn on the forehand, the horse rotates around a pivot point, which is the front leg of the direction of the turn. In a turn on the forehand to the left, the pivot point is the left front leg, the horse is bent to the left, and his hindquarters move to the right. As the hindquarters move to the right, the left hind crosses over and in front of the right hind.

Turn on the Hindquarters. When performing the turn on the hindquarters (haunches), the horse should pivot on the inside hind leg and cross the outside front leg over the inside front leg. The turn on the hindquarters is a controlled maneuver done in 4-beat walk time. The most common turns are the quarter turn (90 degrees), half turn (180 degrees), ¾ turn (270 degrees), full turn (360 degrees), and 1¼ turn (360 degrees plus 90 degrees).

Sidepass. In a sidepass, the horse's entire body is straight or very slightly counterflexed, and he steps directly sideways. In a sidepass to the right, the left legs cross over in front of the right legs as the horse moves sideways.

Two-Track. In a two-track, the horse moves forward and sideways on a diagonal line, with the horse's body bent slightly away from the direction in which he is moving.

Leg Yield. In a leg yield, the horse moves forward but steps sideways with the hind legs; the horse is flexed opposite to the direction he is moving.

Simple Change. A simple lead change is a change from one lead at the lope to the other lead at the lope, usually with a halt or a prescribed number of walk or jog strides in between. The change should be executed precisely, with the number of designated strides or steps, and at the designated location. The change should occur smoothly. The horse's body should remain straight before, during, and after the change.

Flying Change. A flying lead change is a change in the air, between 2 lope strides, from one lead to the other lead with the change occurring simultaneously with the front and rear legs. The change should be executed smoothly, with the horse's body straight, and at the designated location.

Counter-Canter. The counter-canter is a prescribed, balanced lope on one lead while the horse is traveling in a curve in the opposite direction. For example, when you ask the horse to lope on the right lead in a circle to the left, you are asking him to counter-canter. When counter-cantering, there should be no change in rhythm or stride and the horse should be bent toward the lead, not the curve.

Any Other Maneuver. In some rule books, this phrase is included to allow the judge to add any other maneuver to the pattern that he or she deems appropriate.

Ride without Stirrups. In most rule books, it is permissible for the judge to require the riders to perform any pattern without stirrups. In Western Horsemanship, the empty stirrups hang freely along the horse's sides. In some instances, riding without stirrups is prohibited for riders younger than a certain age.

USUALLY NOT ALLOWED

Although popular in the past, the following tests are not often asked for due to concerns with safety and time restrictions.

Asking Riders to Mount or Dismount. Due to the time it would require for an entire class of riders to dismount and mount and the difficulty some younger riders have mounting larger horses, mounting and dismounting may be a prohibited test in your rule book.

Asking Riders to Exchange Horses. A test of true horsemanship is to see a rider perform well on another exhibitor's horse. However, due to safety and liability concerns, this test is usually prohibited.

STEPS AND STRIDE FOR GAITS AND MANEUVERS

GAIT OR MANEUVER	NUMBER OF STEPS	LENGTH OF STRIDE (AVERAGE)
Walk	4	5½' (1.7 m)
Jog	2	8' (2.4 m)
Extended jog	2	10' (3.1 m)
Lope	3	10' (3.1 m)
Extended lope	3	12' (3.7 m)
Gallop	4	12' (3.7 m)
Back	2	4½' (1.4 m)
Turn on the forehand, turn on the hindquarters	4	N/A
Sidepass	2	N/A

NUMBER OF STRIDES IN VARIOUS SIZED CIRCLES

DIAMETER	CIRCUMFERENCE	NUMBER OF STRIDES (AVERAGE)
20' (6.1 m)	63' (19.2 m)	11 at walk 8 at jog 6 at lope
30' (9.2 m)	94' (28.7 m)	17 at walk 12 at jog 9 at lope
50' (15.3 m)	157' (47.9 m)	29 at walk 20 at jog 16 at lope
66' (20.1 m)	207' (63.1 m)	38 at walk 26 at jog 21 at lope

Beginning Western Horsemanship Patterns

Beginning patterns are suitable for any rider just starting out. They require the basic gaits: walk, jog, lope, stop, and back. There are no simple or flying lead changes and no extended gaits. In the most elementary classes, only the walk, jog, and stop are included. Later, the jog to lope transition is added; finally, the walk to lope transition is included. Turning is minimal and involves large circles or gentle serpentines.

At home, a rider of any age can practice a beginning pattern and benefit from it. Besides performing the required maneuvers, you can focus on exactly where your gait transitions take place; your aids to achieve the transitions; your position during the entire pattern; and your horse's consistency in frame, rhythm, and stride length.

On the following page, you'll find four blank arenas where you can record patterns that you've ridden at shows.

TRAINING NOTES
_____
_____
_____
_____
_____
_____
_____
_____
_____
_____
_____
_____
_____
_____
_____
_____
_____
_____
_____
_____
_____
_____
_____

COMPETITION GOALS
_____
_____
_____
_____
_____
_____
_____
_____
_____
_____
_____
_____
_____
_____
_____
_____
_____
_____
_____
_____
_____
_____
_____

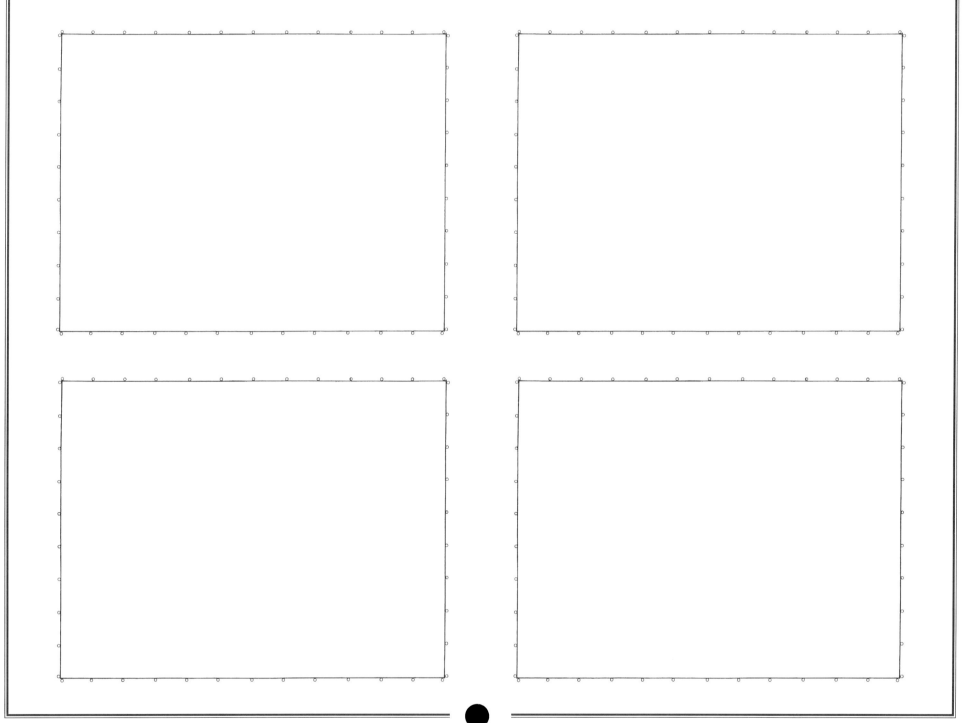

PATTERN 1

A   Jog

B   Turn

C   Stop

Stand for 3 seconds

Walk

Join new lineup

Pattern Help

Since this is a beginning pattern that is suitable for 4-H, I suggest you line your horse up so that he is staring down the pattern line just like the horse in the drawing. His front feet should be about 5 feet (1.5 m) from cone A; the tips of his ears about 3 feet (0.9 m) from the cone.

When the judge looks at you and it is time for you to go, squeeze your horse's ribs with both legs to ask him to walk.

As soon as he starts at the walk, squeeze him again, harder, for the jog. This should result in his walking about 3 to 4 steps (1 stride) before he starts jogging. He should be jogging when you pass cone A.

A Jog. Keep cone A on your right side. A jog is a 2-beat diagonal gait that is quiet and balanced. You want your horse to jog with energy, but you don't want him to jog fast or with a long stride because it will be hard for you to sit well and to make a smooth turn. Head straight toward cone B, but turn one-half horse length before you get to it; 2 to 3 strides before cone B, gather your thoughts and your horse, but not so much that you cause him to walk. (See Pattern 9.)

B Turn left. Turning should be a smooth, continuous arc. The horse should not speed up, slow down, or get stiff.

Use a neck rein on the right side of your horse's neck; weight your left seat bone; bring your right shoulder forward. When you are halfway through the turn, begin straightening or you will overturn. Head straight forward and look to the next marker. You want to stop with cone C on your right. (See Patterns 3, 6, and 16.)

C Stop. To stop your horse, as you approach cone C, sit deep in the saddle, look straight ahead, increase pressure on the reins by squeezing your fist or pulling straight back slightly, about 1 to 2 inches (2.5–5.1 cm) at the most, making sure your hand stays in front of or above the saddle horn. Take care not to let your hand drift off to the left or the right as this might make your horse stop crooked. (See Pattern 3.)

Stand for 3 seconds. Once your horse has stopped, you should release your active aids. Relax your legs and seat, and release a little contact on the reins. You want the horse to be in "neutral," so your aids should be "neutral," too. (See Tip below.)

Walk. When 3 seconds are up, squeeze with both legs to cause your horse to walk. As soon as he takes the first few steps, begin turning him to the right. After you've walked a few steps, the pattern is over and the judge will be watching the next exhibitor. (See Pattern 8.)

Join the new lineup. Although this portion of the pattern is not being judged, you still want to maneuver properly. If you are the first in the lineup, stop your horse parallel to the rail such that the resulting line won't cause problems with those that are performing the pattern. If you are next in line, "park" your horse parallel to the first horse but with adequate space between you for safety. If you and the other rider reached out your arms toward each other and they touched, you would be too close.

TIP COUNTING 3 SECONDS

It is up to you to determine how long 3 seconds are; the judge is not responsible for telling you. Say to yourself, in your mind, without moving your lips, "One thousand one. One thousand two. One thousand three." And it will be close enough to 3 seconds.

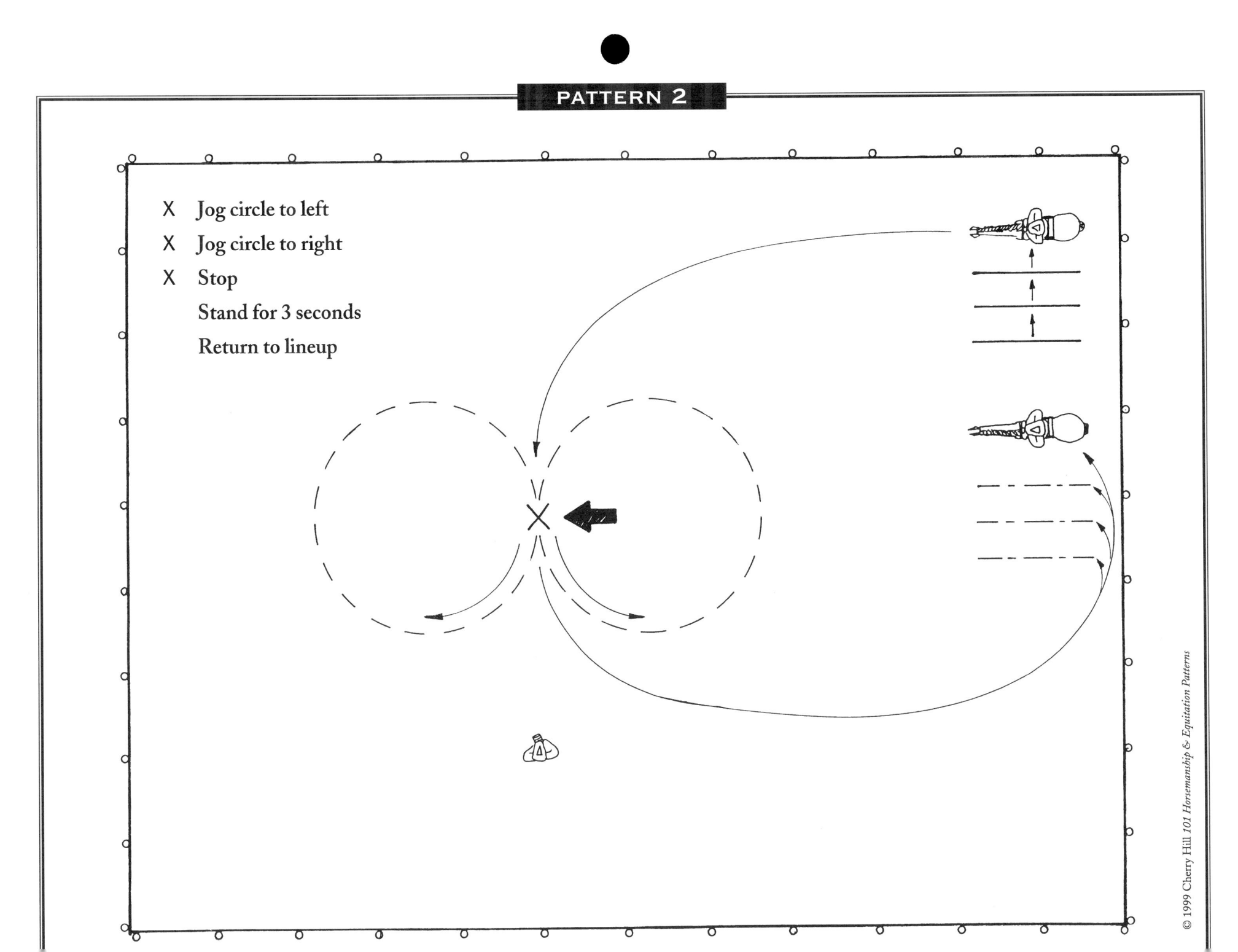

PATTERN 2

X Jog circle to left
X Jog circle to right
X Stop
   Stand for 3 seconds
   Return to lineup

Pattern Help

This pattern is suitable for beginning 4-H riders. It begins and ends at X, an imaginary point at the center of the figure 8. It is up to you to decide how to get to X and leave X. That portion of the pattern is not judged, but you still should be riding as if it were.

Safety is emphasized. Sometimes the judge will require one exhibitor to be completely finished before the next rider begins to go on course. In other shows, the judge needs to keep things moving along and needs the riders to be ready. If the show is moving quickly, start your horse moving out of the lineup when the previous rider has finished the 3-second stand and is returning to the lineup. I suggest you walk out of the lineup, jog to X, and continue jogging. Often in this type of pattern, there are no cones to help or hinder you. You will use the position of the judge as a reference point for the center of your figure 8.

X Jog circle to the left. This means to *your* left, not the judge's. Be sure to know your left from your right because even if you ride beautifully, if you go to the right first it will cost you points. As you finish your left circle, try to ride your horse straight for 1 to 2 straight strides before you start the right circle. (See Pattern 9.)

X Jog circle to the right. Try to match the size of the circle that you rode to the left. (See Patterns 3, 6, 16, and 18.)

X Stop. (See Pattern 3.)

Stand for 3 seconds. (See Pattern 1.) When 3 seconds are up, you can **leave the pattern by walking, jogging, or loping back to the lineup.** However, when you get close to the lineup, be sure to drop down to the walk so that you don't disrupt the other horses.

TIP SIZE AND SHAPE OF CIRCLES

In a pattern like this, there are no cones to indicate the size of the circles. Therefore, unless the judge tells you otherwise before the class begins, you could ride any size circles you want. Bigger circles require less sharp turning and are easier for beginning riders or stiffer horses, but they take longer to ride. Smaller circles are quicker to ride because you are covering less ground, but the horse must be collected and flexible in order to bend more sharply.

It doesn't matter that you know how large in feet (or meters) the circle is that you are going to make. What you need to know is what size circle you can make *smoothly.* And you must be able to make the same size circle in both directions. Some horses are stiffer in one direction and want to make a huge circle, but in the other direction they want to curl up and make a tiny circle. You need to make both circles the same size and shape. A circle should be uniformly round, not egg shaped or oblong or flat on one side.

PATTERN 3*

Stock Seat under 11

A Jog

B Turn left

X Jog left circle

X Jog right circle

X Stop

Back

PATTERN HELP

The cones might be set outside the arena rail (as in Pattern 4) so that they are out of the way for the rail work later. If the cones are outside the arena or if markers are placed on the rail for A and B, just glance at their approximate position as you ride by. If you turn your head and upper body extremely to see where they are located, you could cause your horse to wobble instead of jogging in a straight line.

A Jog. (See Pattern 9.)

B Turn left. (See Tip at right and Patterns 6 and 16.)

X Jog left circle. (See Patterns 2 and 18.)

X Jog right circle. (See Patterns 2 and 18.)

X Stop. You don't want to surprise your jogging horse with a sudden pull on the reins for a stop. Prepare him for the stop:

★ Keep your upper body straight.

★ Still your seat; don't follow the movement of the jog anymore.

★ Keep both of your legs on the horse's sides at the cinch.

★ Shorten your reins by creeping up the reins with your fingers or move your reining hand straight backward 1 to 2 inches (2.5–5.1 cm). Be sure your reining hand is in front of or above the saddle horn.

★ As soon as the horse has "started to stop," begin easing the aids.

Back. A back is a 2-beat diagonal gait in reverse. (See Pattern 7.)

This pattern ends after the back, so when you have finished backing, stop your horse and look at the judge. The judge will often nod to you, telling you that you are finished and to make room for the next rider. The ring steward will tell you where to go after you complete this pattern.

TIP **TURNING**

To make a controlled left turn at cone B, imagine you are turning in the corner of an arena:

- Start the turn one-half horse length before the cone.
- Move your right shoulder forward; this will cause more weight to be on your left seat bone.
- Deepen your left knee and keep your heel down to prevent your left side from collapsing.
- Look slightly to the left as you turn.
- Use your left leg at the cinch to help bend the horse.
- Use your right leg slightly behind the cinch to keep the horse's hindquarters on the line.
- Move your reining hand to the left 1 to 2 inches (2.5–5.1 cm) at the most.

C   B   A

D   E

A   Walk

B   Jog

C   Lope left lead

D   Walk

E   Stop

Back 4 steps

Pattern Help

A Walk. (See Patterns 5 and 8.)

B Jog. (See Pattern 6.)

C Lope left lead. To ask your horse to lope, use two sets of aids: first, a set of positioning aids, then the aids for the lope. For the positioning aids, you want to get the horse ready for the lead you want. For the left lead, you want to shift your horse's weight over to the right side of his body momentarily. If you move his weight over to the right side of his body for a fraction of a second, you are lightening his left side, which will make it easier for him to take the left lead. You do this mainly by momentarily weighting your left seat bone and applying your left leg at the cinch. You might also need to apply a little left neck rein to shift his forehand weight over, too. As soon as you feel he has done this, which should just be 1 second, it's time to use the aids for the lope.

The aids for the lope left lead are:

★ Left seat bone forward with weight in your left stirrup and a lowered knee and heel to position the horse and keep him straight.

★ Right leg behind the cinch with a rolling forward feeling from your right seat bone (which is farther back) to your left seat bone (which is farther forward) to ask for the left lead.

Now that your horse is loping, add the left bend and use your eyes to help you make a nice rounded blue-ribbon U-shape. Plan to make your next transition alongside cone D. (See Tip at right.)

D Walk. (See Pattern 10.)

E Stop. (See Pattern 3.)

Back 4 steps. (See Pattern 7.)

TIP | JOG TO LOPE

To give you an idea of how long it takes to apply the aids for the lope, say, "Position aids, lope," and in the time it takes you to say those words, you should have applied the position aids and then loped. If you take too long with the positioning aids, your horse will "stall out."

This is a fairly sophisticated transition for a beginning rider, but it's best if you learn it correctly. And if you are ready to show, you should know the correct way. That way, in the more advanced patterns you will be able to lope on any lead at any time.

TIP | DETERMINING LEFT LEAD

The left lead lope is a 3-beat gait with the following footfall pattern:

1. Right hind
2. Left hind and right front
3. Left front

When your horse is traveling to the left, he should be on the left lead. His left front leg will reach farther forward than his right front leg. Without moving your head, glance down at your horse's shoulders to see which shoulder is moving farther ahead. That is what lead your horse is on. Register what that feels like in your seat and legs so that later you can tell just by feeling what lead your horse is on.

A Walk 3 strides

Jog

B Lope left lead

C Stop

Back 4 steps

Walk

Return to lineup

PATTERN HELP

A Walk 3 strides, then jog. A walk is a controlled gait with 4 distinct beats. The rhythm of the 4 beats should be even, not hurried in some spots. To ride the walk, sit with a relaxed seat and legs. Let your seat follow the slightly side-to-side and back-to-front movement of the walk, but keep your upper body still. If your horse is walking lazily, dragging his toes, stumbling or just "moseying" along, you will need to squeeze with both legs to energize him. (See Patterns 6 and 8.)

B Lope left lead. (See Pattern 4.)

C Stop. (See Tip at right.)

Back 4 steps. (See Pattern 7.)

Walk. (See Pattern 8.)

Return to the lineup.

TIP LOPE TO STOP

In beginning patterns, a judge would rather see you perform a lope to jog to stop in good form than an abrupt lope to stop in poor form. However, the rider who can perform a lope to stop in good form will earn the most points because this is what is asked for. If you yank abruptly on the reins, you will startle your horse and he will most likely throw his head up, open his mouth to avoid the harsh action of the bit, and stiffen into a very unglamorous stop of sorts. To avoid this, properly prepare your horse by collecting and balancing him 2 to 3 strides before the stop. Shorten the stride of the lope and imagine you are loping uphill as you:

- Keep your upper body straight, with your shoulders over your hips.
- During the portion of the lope stride when your seat is going down, still the motion of your seat; don't continue following the motion of the lope.
- Keep both your legs on the horse's sides at the cinch to keep him straight.
- Shorten the reins 1 to 2 inches (2.5–5.1 cm).
- As soon as the horse has stopped, ease up on your aids.

PATTERN 6

A Walk 2 strides
   Jog
   Turn left
B Jog around cone B
C Lope left lead
D Stop
   Back 4 steps

Pattern Help

A Walk 2 strides. A stride is one complete set of steps. In the walk, 1 stride is a complete 4-beat revolution of the horse's legs: left hind, left front, right hind, right front. To count 2 strides, count every time you feel a particular hind leg reach forward: left hind 1, left hind 2. If you have not developed feel yet, you can glance down at a front leg to measure: left front 1, left front 2. Eventually, you should train yourself to count strides by feel through your seat so that you can most effectively communicate with your horse. (See Pattern 8.)

Jog, then turn left. (See Tip at right.)

B Jog around cone B. As you jog your horse in a gentle bend around the cone, be sure that:

★ His poll stays at a consistent level. If it drops way down, it means he is heavy on his forehand or getting behind the bit. If he raises up, it indicates resistance to your reining aids. His back will become hollow, and you will no longer be able to use your seat aids effectively.

★ He maintains a steady rhythm. If he speeds up, it means he is losing his balance. If he slows down, he is confusing your reining aid for turning with one for slowing down or stopping.

★ As you bend him to the left (making good use of your seat and leg aids), his head, neck and body turn slightly to the left. When you change the bend, his head and neck turn slightly to the right.

C Lope left lead. Be sure to straighten your horse's body and shift the weight over to the right side of his body before you ask for the lope; otherwise, you might get a right lead instead of a left lead. Be sure your lope aids ask for a forward depart. (See Patterns 4 and 19.)

D Stop. (See Pattern 5.)

Back 4 steps. (See Pattern 7.)

TIP | WALK TO JOG

You might think this is almost too simple to worry about, but it is one of the best elementary exercises to start collecting your horse and keeping him straight. When you ask your horse to jog by sitting deep in the saddle, squeezing with both legs at or slightly behind the cinch, and giving a little forward with your reining hand, he should energetically reach under with his hind legs and lift his back. You should feel yourself rise a little as he takes off. This is a good sign. If your horse's back stays flat or caves in when he starts to jog, you need to practice lots of these transitions to teach him how to round up underneath you. He needs to learn to jog up energetically, lift his back, and keep his body straight. Keep your mind in the middle and a leg on each side.

A Jog
     Lope left lead

B Turn left

C Stop
     Back 4 steps
     Walk
     Return to lineup

B

A

C

Pattern Help

A Jog until halfway between cones A and B. (See Pattern 9.)

Then lope left lead. (See Patterns 4 and 19.)

B Turn left. This is a sharp turn! (See Pattern 15.)

C Stop. (See Pattern 5.)

Back 4 steps.

After the stop, drive your horse up to the bit using your seat and legs. You want him to lean his body forward without stepping forward. Just as he "arrives" at the bit, he should flex at the poll and jaw and round his back. Before he takes a step forward, relax your rein contact somewhat but keep your seat and leg aids driving, and he will back softly.

When your horse backs, he should pick up two legs at a time (right front and left hind) and reach backward with them and set them down. As he is setting them down, the other diagonal pair (left front and right hind) will lift, reach back, and set down. If a horse drags his feet backward through the dirt, it shows the horse is very lazy and has not been taught to step backward with energy. If a horse takes very tiny steps backward, it means he is being resistant to the rider's aids. A horse should not be stiff in the jaw, nor should he be "pulled" backward with rein pressure.

It is easy to count 4 steps while backing. Every time your horse picks up one diagonal pair of legs and moves it back, you will feel it in your hips. Your pelvis will rock back and forth from side to side as he backs. You can count something like this: "Left rear 1, right rear 2, left rear 3, right rear 4." And that would be the 4 steps back. If you need to look at the shoulder to learn how to feel, you can count like this: "Left front 1, right front 2, left front 3, right front 4." And that would be the 4 steps.

Walk and return to the lineup.

TIP **BEING FACED WITH A CHALLENGING PATTERN**

If you are a novice rider and you arrive at a show to find this pattern for your class, you might think it's pretty easy and you can just cruise. But let me point out that this beginning pattern has one very advanced maneuver in it. It is the sharp turn at cone B at the lope. To perform this well, you will need to have your horse collected and you will have to plan ahead so that after you have turned you are on a straight line toward the judge with cone C on your right. The most common error here would be to turn too late or too wide and end making a curved line that is way on the other side of cone C. (See Pattern 15 for more help with this tricky maneuver.)

Walk to cone **A**

A Jog

B Lope left lead

Lope balloon

C Stop

Back 4 steps

Walk

Exit arena at any gait

C

B

A

Pattern Help

Walk to cone A. Be ready in the lineup so that as the rider before you is finishing, your horse is attentive and ready to walk. This takes practice and timing. If you get your horse "too ready," he might walk or turn in anticipation and you will have a poor start. (See Tip at right.)

A Jog. Begin the jog as soon as your horse's head passes cone A. Remember, cone A is to your left. As you jog toward cone B, remember to keep it to your right. Just as your horse's head passes cone B, you should lope. That means you must prepare your horse 1 stride before with the positioning aids. (See Pattern 6.)

B Lope left lead. The lope depart should be prompt and the horse's body should be straight. (See Patterns 4 and 19.)

Lope balloon. This shape is a circle with a triangle top on it, so I call it a balloon. You will lope your horse for 1 or 2 strides straight before you begin the circle portion. During the circle work, be mentally prepared for what is coming 3 to 4 strides ahead. As you finish the circle portion, you again want to plan ahead so that when you straighten you will be heading on a straight line that will pass right next to cone C, with cone C on your right. As you are loping the final straightaway, be sure your horse's body is absolutely straight by having even contact on your six points: two reins, two seat bones, and two legs. Gather him slightly, but not too much or he might jog.

C Stop. (See Pattern 5.)

Back 4 steps. (See Pattern 7.)

Walk. (See Tip below.)

Exit the arena at any gait. This means you can exit the arena at the gait of your choice: a walk, jog, or lope. Choose a gait that you feel is safe for you. You don't want to choose the lope if you think your horse will get excited when he sees the open gate and bolt out of the arena. On the other hand, walking out of a big arena will take quite a bit of time, which might delay the next rider from starting.

At the end of the pattern, after the back, you need to show the judge that you can calmly walk your horse a few strides after the lope, stop, and back to demonstrate that you have control of your horse and can calmly walk away. You will need to do this on light contact. If you have to hold the horse strongly with the rein, it shows a lack of practice.

TIP | WALK

The walk is baby stuff, right? Wrong. The halt to walk at the beginning and end of this pattern are important indicators of your ability as a rider. It can be difficult to take a quiet, relaxed horse out of a lineup where he is comfortably standing next to other horses and have him walk off straight and with energy. Practice this at home. Stop your horse and have him stand for several minutes, then walk him off. Do this many times so that you'll see how much leg and seat are necessary. Sometimes you might be standing in a horsemanship lineup for 15 minutes or more before it is your turn.

PATTERN 9

B ⊙   **A** ⊙

C ●   ⊙ **D**

E ●

F ⊙

G ⊙

A Jog

B Turn left

C Lope left lead

    Lope circle

E Jog

F Turn right

G Stop

    Back 4 steps

    Join new lineup

PATTERN HELP

A Jog. To obtain maximum credit, you will have your horse positioned with his head at cone A when the last rider is just finishing her back. That way when the judge looks your way, you can take off from a halt to a jog instantly. This is easier said than done. (See Tip below.)

B Turn left. Prepare your horse before cone B by deepening your seat and gathering your horse in with the reins just a tad but not so much that he walks. Begin the turn about 1 stride before you get to cone B. (See Patterns 3, 6, and 16.)

C Lope left lead. There is no cone at C, so you will have to use your judgment, making allowances for everything that has to happen between cones B and F. Lope at C with the horse's body straight and *then* turn into the left circle. (See Patterns 4 and 19.)

Lope a circle between C and D. Be sure to note that the circle is to be made inside cone D. A very common error is to lope outside the cone. Sometimes it's your horse's idea because he wants to be close to the lineup. Be aware that he is likely to break to a trot at D and veer toward the other horses. Finish the circle at the same point you started or you might run out of room before you get to E. (See Patterns 2 and 18.)

Lope to E. E is also an imaginary point. If you've planned things right, after the circle, you should have room to straighten your horse for at least 2 strides before you make the downward transition to the jog.

E Jog. You should have room to jog your horse for at least 2 strides before you must turn. (See Pattern 13.)

F Turn right and continue jogging. (See Patterns 3, 6, and 16.)

G Stop. (See Pattern 3.)

Back 4 steps. (See Pattern 7.)

Walk. (See Pattern 8.)

Join the new lineup.

TIP HALT TO JOG

To start your pattern off with a sparkle, you should perfect the halt-to-jog transition. It's fun! Think "Spring into action, my steed!" as you apply the following aids:

- Maintain contact with the reins as you would in a halt.
- Hug the horse's sides and abdominals with your lower legs to cause him to lift his back and get light.
- Then apply intermittent "squeeze, squeeze, squeeze" with your legs as you lighten your seat, and you'll likely be off in a princely jog.

The reason you need to maintain contact with the reins (unlike *giving* with the reins as you do for a halt-to-walk transition) is that you want the horse to strike off energized, somewhat collected, and round right off the bat. You don't want him to lower his head and neck too much, so you "keep him on the aids" for takeoff.

A Jog

B Lope right lead

Lope circle

Walk

C Stop

Back 4 steps

Walk

Find a place on rail

Pattern Help

A Jog. (See Pattern 9.)

B Lope right lead. You have two things happening at once: a lope depart right lead and a circle. Separate them into two distinct elements: a forward, straight lope depart on the right lead, *then* a circle. Say to yourself, "Positioning aids, lope" at the same time you apply the aids. For right lead positioning aids, move the horse's weight to the left. Immediately apply the aids for the lope. The aids for the lope right lead are:

★ Right seat bone forward with weight in your right stirrup and a lowered knee and heel

★ Left leg behind the cinch with a rolling forward feeling from your left seat bone (which is farther back) to your right seat bone (which is farther forward)

The right lead lope is a 3-beat gait with the following footfall pattern: (1) left hind, (2) right hind and left front, and (3) right front. When your horse is traveling to the right, he should be on the right lead. His right front leg will reach farther forward than his left front leg. Without moving your head, glance down at your horse's shoulders to see which shoulder is moving farther ahead. That is what lead your horse is on. Register what that feels like in your seat and legs so that later you can tell just by feeling what lead your horse is on. (See Patterns 4 and 19.)

Lope a circle to the right. After the lope depart, begin bending your horse to the right and plan the circle size by a quick glance with your eyes. Be sure to start and finish the circle at cone B. There are no markers to indicate size. Choose the size circle that your horse can lope without speeding up, breaking to a jog, or stiffening. Usually a 50-foot (15.3 m) diameter circle works well. (See Patterns 2 and 18.)

Walk. Going from a lope to a walk at the same time you are finishing a circle and starting a straight line can be tricky. (See Tip below.)

C Stop.

Back 4 steps. (See Pattern 7.)

Walk. (See Patterns 5 and 8.)

Find a place on the rail.

TIP **LOPE TO WALK**

In some ways, this is a more challenging transition than a lope to stop. You need to finish the circle at the lope with your horse still bent to the right. As you join the straight line, you will have to use slightly more right neck rein (to cause the horse to move his neck to the left) and right leg behind the cinch to straighten your horse. At the same time you will need to move your left leg into a neutral central position. Shorten the lope for 2 to 3 strides, then still the motion in your seat for a brief instant as you draw your reining hand about 1 inch (2.5 cm) back toward your belt buckle. When you feel the horse breaking down from the lope, get an even feel on both reins and begin the following motion of your seat to a 4-beat walk. If you get a stride of jog in between, keep your cool and get down to a walk as soon as possible, but with smooth application of the aids. I'd find it much less of an error if the transition were totally smooth and had 1 jog stride in between the lope and walk than if the horse stopped abruptly and had to be urged on to walk. Of course, the ideal is a smooth transition directly from a lope to a forward, straight walk. This takes lots of at-home practice.

C

B

A

D

E

Jog

After cone C, lope left lead

Lope circle

Walk

Stop

Back 4 steps

Find a place on rail

PATTERN HELP

Jog from the lineup around cone A. (See Pattern 9.)

Jog around cone B. (See Patterns 3, 6, and 16.)

Jog to cone C. In a change of bend pattern like this, you are making a shallow serpentine around cones to demonstrate that your horse bends easily in both directions. The judge will be looking for an evenness in rhythm, a consistent head carriage, and a symmetric shape. If the horse quickens the jog, breaks to a walk, throws his head up or twists it when being reined, veers out to one side, or makes a close shave to a cone or a huge side trip away from a cone (both indicating he is not supple), you will lose credit.

After cone C, lope left lead. Make it your goal to pass cone C with your horse's body as straight as possible. This will make it easier for you to prepare for the left lope depart by shifting the horse's weight over to his right side. If the horse is already turning left when you apply your lope positioning aids, you will have a harder time moving his weight off to the right. (See Patterns 4 and 19.)

Lope a circle to the left keeping cone D to your left. Here is a pattern that indicates the cone is to be on the *inside* of the circle. Be sure it is! (See Patterns 2 and 18.)

Finish the circle.

When straight, walk. (See Pattern 10.)

Stop.

Back 4 steps. (See Pattern 7.)

Find a place on the rail. The pattern ended with the back steps, so theoretically you can go to the rail any way you want. I suggest turning your horse to the right so you can make an arc around cone E. Walk a few steps, then jog into place. Break down to a walk before you get too close to other exhibitors who might already be on the rail.

TIP NECK REINING

Ah, the art of neck reining. I'm afraid it's getting harder to find a horse that really neck reins light and equally well in both directions. Why? Because it takes time. If you really want to make a judge's heart sing, take the time to make your horse's neck reining really solid. Here's some help.

In neck reining, the horse is taught to turn away from the touch of the rein on his neck. When the rein touches the right side of the neck, the horse turns left. The horse is taught this association by using seat and legs and two hands and a snaffle bit. If your horse needs a tune-up, go back to the snaffle and two hands. When you lay the rein on the right side of the horse's neck, draw your left shoulder back, weight your left seat bone, and let your left leg hang at or slightly behind the cinch. Let your right shoulder move forward and apply your right leg at or in front of the cinch at the same time you use the left rein with a slightly outward and backward pull to guide the horse through the turn. Gradually use less and less left rein; eventually the horse turns left just from your seat and leg aids and the touch of the right rein on his neck. A neck rein is designed to be used lightly. If you use it too strongly, it would give the horse the opposite signal than is desired. If you use the right neck rein very strongly, it will actually pull the horse's nose to the right and backward, making it difficult to impossible for the horse to turn left!

C

B

A

D

E

A Jog

B Walk

C Lope left lead

D Jog

E Stop

Back 4 steps

PATTERN HELP

A Jog. (See Pattern 9.)

B Walk. Jog to walk is the other half of that great elementary collection exercise in Pattern 6. To perfect the jog-to-walk transition, you're going to have to practice this a lot at home. In this pattern, because you barely get started jogging before you have to walk, you must be certain you can do these things in short order. The key to getting a forward walk from a jog is that as soon as you feel your horse "begin to stop jogging," you need to release your restraining aids. Here's what I mean:

★ Quit following the jog with your seat; still your seat.

★ Shorten the reins with crawling fingers or draw your reining hand back toward your belt buckle about 1 inch (2.5 cm). Be sure to keep your reining hand in front of the saddle horn.

★ Immediately when you feel your horse get the signal to "power down a notch," you must:

> Move your reining hand forward toward your horse's mane about 1 to 2 inches (2.5–5.1 cm) to allow your horse to lower and reach with his neck for the walk.

> Initiate and follow the 4-beat walk tempo with your seat.

> Keep your legs evenly on your horse to keep him straight.

C Lope left lead. (See Tip at right.)

D Jog. (See Pattern 13.)

E Stop. (See Pattern 3.)

Back 4 steps. (See Pattern 7.)

TIP WALK TO LOPE

This should be a piece of cake. You have already been practicing the jog-to-lope transition, and you understand that you need to first apply positioning aids and then immediately the lope aids. The same goes here. The only difference is that now you must also apply a little more gusto in the impulsion department to get your horse to strike off into a clean lope. And you need to hone your precision so that everything runs like clockwork. Be sure you look foward during the transition. If you let your eyes drop, you will tend to weight your horse's forehand at a time when it especially needs to be light.

For a walk to lope left lead, first shift your horse's weight over to his right side: your left leg should be at the cinch, and possibly give a little left neck rein. Instantly, when you feel the weight shift, apply the lope aids: your right seat bone and leg should be deep and slightly behind the cinch, sending energy rolling diagonally forward to your left seat bone, which is slightly ahead of your right seat bone.

It's time to say something about your shoulder and lope departs. Generally, your shoulders will automatically be over your hips, so if your right seat bone is back your right shoulder will be slightly back. For the left lope depart, your left shoulder would be slightly ahead of the right shoulder for the depart but as soon as the lope is established the shoulders should once more be even. Try to keep your shoulders even most of the time. Never use exaggerated upper body twists to try to accomplish lope departs or other maneuvers. And be ever-vigilant to prevent a dropped shoulder — one that dips lower than the other — as this collapses that whole side of your body and makes even seat bone contact and balanced riding impossible.

A

A Walk 3 strides

Lope left lead

B Jog

C Stop

Back 4 steps

Walk

Return to lineup

B

C

PATTERN HELP

A Walk 3 strides. The key here is 3 strides, which are equal to 12 steps or about 16 feet (4.9 m). Start your count as soon as your horse's ears pass the cone. Note that the cone is outside the arena. This allows the rail work to follow the pattern work without necessitating moving cones out of the way. (See Patterns 5 and 8.)

Lope left lead. There isn't a marker, but the depart should take place after 3 strides of walk. Try your best to design the lope depart to occur on a straight line as it will be much easier to get a nice, balanced lope, and one that is on the correct lead, if you are not turning. When you turn, aim to pass close to cone B with it on your right side. (See Pattern 12.)

B Jog. (See Tip at right for the transition.) As you jog, try to make the curve shape of this half of the pattern be a mirror image of the curve you and your horse created in the first half of the pattern. We are looking for symmetry!

C Stop. (See Pattern 3.)

Back 4 steps. (See Pattern 7.)

Walk.

Return to the lineup.

<table>
<tr><td>TIP</td><td>LOPE TO JOG</td></tr>
</table>

In a downward transition from a lope to a jog on a straight line, your seat bones, shoulders, and legs should be fairly even and symmetrical. If anything, in this left lead pattern, your left shoulder and seat bone might be slightly ahead of their right counterparts, but if they are more than 1 or 2 inches (2.5 or 5.1 cm) ahead, that is undesirable. Also, your right leg will be slightly behind the cinch. To prepare for the downward transition to a balanced, symmetrical jog, you will want to "square up"; that is, move your right leg up to the cinch so that it's directly across from your left leg, even up your shoulders, and be sure you feel weight evenly on your seat bones. Quit following the 3-beat lope rhythm with your seat. Maintain a still seat, flex your abdominals, and move your reining hand about 1 inch (2.5 cm) toward your belt buckle. As soon as the horse jogs, yield with your reining hand slightly and follow the 2-beat jog with your seat.

E

D

C

B

A

A Walk 2 strides

Jog

Lope right lead

E Stop

Back 4 steps

Pattern Help

A Walk 2 strides. That's 8 beats, or about 11 feet (3.4 m). If you find that it's impossible to fit 2 strides into this pattern as drawn, you have several options. If you have time before the class begins, you can ask the ring steward for clarification or ask if the cone is properly placed. If you ask the question respectfully, you might find that an error *was* made and the cone might be repositioned. However, if the class has begun and it is apparent that no rider is going to be able to fit 2 strides in, you have two choices. Either walk 1 stride and begin your serpentine on time or walk 2 strides and begin your serpentine late. Choose the option that will work best with your horse. It would be hard for me to predict which way the judge at your show might rule, but I'd suggest walking one full stride, then squeezing your horse into a jog while you begin your serpentine. Be sure to keep your poise about any inconveniences like this. (See Patterns 5 and 8.)

Jog. (See Pattern 6.)

Jog around cone B. (See Patterns 3, 6, and 16.)

Jog around cone C. (See Pattern 11.)

Between cones C and D, lope right lead. This has a few tricky aspects to it. Technically you should ask for the lope on the small "straightaway" between the loops around cones C and D. At that one moment, the horse is straight, not bending right or left. He has just finished bending left and after the lope will bend right. Should you ask for the lope slightly ahead of or after the straightaway? You should know by now that your pre-lope positioning aid shifts the weight of the horse momentarily away from the lead you will be asking for. So in this case, since you'll be asking for a right lead, you will position the horse's weight off to the left before you give the lope aids. That means it would make sense to position your horse for the lope just before the straightaway while he is just finishing up a left bend, as this will help you shift his weight to the left. Then you can ask for the right lead in the straightaway, and voilà! You're on the way to the blue ribbon. If instead you position the horse in the straightaway and then ask for the lope when you start turning right, you might have an awkward surprise. (See Patterns 4 and 19.)

E Stop. (See Pattern 5.)

Back 4 steps. (See Pattern 7.)

TIP STEPPING OFF CONES

When cones are set up, many judges and ring stewards step off distances to place cones. One stride, or 2 energetic steps, equals 5 to 6 feet (1.5–1.8 m). This is a pretty good "guesstimate" for people of average height. If you are much shorter or taller than 5 feet 6 inches (1.7 m) to 5 feet 10 inches (1.8 m), you'll need to check your stride length. Set cones up at home for practice. Cones set farther apart are asking for forward transitions and forward, energetic gaits. Cones set closer together require collection and precision and can cause a large horse, especially, to have "backward" transitions.

PATTERN 15

A   Jog

B   Lope left lead

C   Turn around cone

D   Walk

E   Lope right lead

F   Stop

   Back 4 steps

   Find a place on rail,
     tracking right

Pattern Help

A Jog. This pattern might be run with all cones as shown here or with minimal cones or no cones. You might see a ribbon tied on the rail for cone A, a cone at C, and the judge standing as cone F. The rest would be up to you to plan. Choose a path 6 feet (1.8 m) from cones A, B, and C. This will give you better position and more room when you get to the turn at cone C. (See Pattern 9.)

B Lope left lead. (See Patterns 4 and 19.)

C Turn around cone. (See Tip at right.)

D Walk. (See Pattern 10.)

E Lope right lead. (See Pattern 10.)

F Stop. (See Pattern 5.)

Back 4 steps. The pattern ends with the back. The judging is completed. Walk forward after the back for 1 or 2 strides, then head to a place on the rail. Be aware of where the judge is standing so that you don't block his or her line of vision to the next exhibitor who is probably already on course. (See Pattern 7.)

Find a place on the rail, tracking right. It is customary for riders to line up on the rail tracking left, that is, making left turns. However, in this particular pattern, the instructions say to track right. If you are the first rider to complete your pattern, be sure you know what that means! You wouldn't want to start confusion with some riders facing one way and some another!

TIP TURN SHARP AROUND CONE AT LOPE

You've loped around the corner of an arena many times, but this turn around cone C is twice as sharp. You won't be loping fast and the goal is not to "kiss" the cone as in barrel racing, but you do want to stay relatively tight around the cone to demonstrate your skill and control. To do this, you will intensify your normal "cornering techniques." Begin the turn aids when you are about one horse length from cone C. When you're loping left and you ride deep into an arena corner, your aids are:

• Sit deep on your left seat bone; with left shoulder back and right shoulder forward.

• Lower your left heel and knee.

• Bend your horse to the left with a right neck rein, but prevent him from overbending and popping his right shoulder out in a bulge.

• Pick up slightly on the reins to collect your horse and elevate his forehand for the turn.

• Use your left leg at the cinch to give the horse a point to bend around.

• Use your right leg to guide the horse around the cone and have it ready slightly behind the cinch to prevent the hindquarters from swinging off the track to the right.

To turn around cone C at a lope left lead, use the same aids but at double intensity for the 2 or 3 strides going into and around the cone. Look to cone D before you start your turn at cone C. Relax the aids as you are coming out of the turn or you will be barrel racing!

Intermediate Western Horsemanship Patterns

Intermediate patterns include everything in beginning patterns plus simple lead changes, 90- or 180-degree turns on the hindquarters, and extended gaits. Hindquarter turns should be forward, light, and tight. Lead changes should be forward and smooth. Gait extensions must show a definite increase in length of stride. Intermediate riders are expected to execute the maneuvers with more precision, accuracy, and promptness than beginning riders. In addition, intermediate riders are expected to perform with a great deal of poise and in a consistent form.

On the following page, you'll find four blank arenas where you can record patterns that you've ridden at shows.

TRAINING NOTES

COMPETITION GOALS

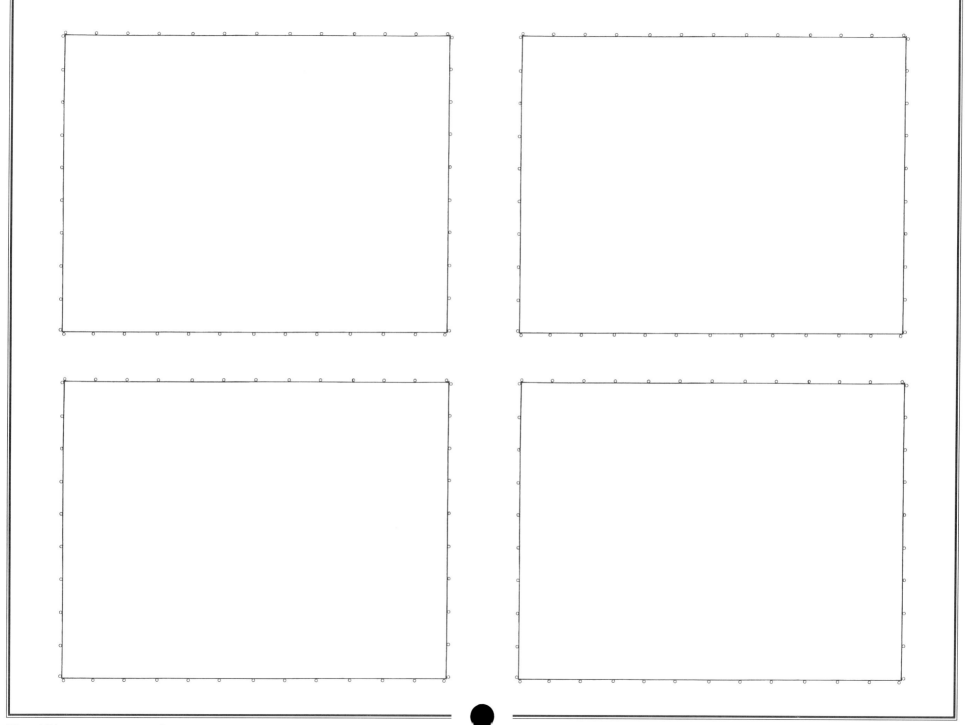

Suitable for AHSA Stock Seat Maiden Novice and Limit classes up to 18 years

B

A

A Jog

B Turn left

Lope left lead

X Simple change

Lope right circle

X Simple change

Lope left circle

X Stop

Pattern Help

A Jog. Prepare for the turn one horse length before cone B. (See Pattern 9.)

B Turn left. As you are turning the corner, keep in mind that right after the corner, you will need to lope. So use the corner to your advantage to position your horse. Use a strong left leg and left seat bone to bend your horse to the left and keep the horse's weight up on the right side of his body in the turn. Then, when it's time to lope left lead, you will already have your horse in position. If you let your horse fall into the left in the turn, you will have to work pretty hard to "lift him up" to get him balanced for the lope depart. A lot of horses like to over-curl to the left, so be on the lookout for this tendency in your horse. (See Patterns 3, 6, and 16.)

Lope left lead. Prepare for the lead change 2 to 3 strides before X. (See Patterns 4 and 19.)

X Simple change to right lead. (See Tip at right.)

Lope right circle. (See Patterns 2 and 18.)

X Simple change to left lead.

Lope left circle. (See Patterns 2 and 18.)

X Stop. After you have paused for several seconds, you should jog or lope out of the center and proceed as directed by the ring steward. (See Pattern 5.)

Note: This pattern does not contain a back, so it will be called for in the lineup or during group rail work. (See Pattern 39.)

TIP | SIMPLE CHANGE

A simple change is a change from one lead at the lope to the other lead at the lope usually with a halt or a prescribed number of walk or jog steps or strides in between. The change should be executed precisely, with the exact number of designated strides or steps and at the designated location. The change should occur smoothly. The horse's body should remain straight before, during, and after the change.

When a simple lead change is called for, it should be a simple lead change, not a flying lead change. (See Pattern 33.)

This pattern does not specify whether the change is to take place through a halt, walk, or jog so the decision is up to each exhibitor. It also does not specify the number of steps or strides in between the leads, so that, too, is up to the exhibitor, but no more than 3 strides should ever be used. You might want to ask the judge what s/he prefers. Suggestions are:

- Lope–halt–position–lope
- Lope–walk 2 strides while positioning–lope
- Lope–jog 2 strides while positioning–lope

PATTERN 17

B   A

C

D

A   Walk

B   Jog

C   Lope right lead

D   Jog

C   Lope left lead

B   Stop

    Back 4 steps

    Find a place on rail

Pattern Help

A Walk. Start your horse out like you are really walking somewhere. You have a lot of ground to cover, and if your horse is pokey at the walk, it will be painfully obvious to you how long it will take to get to B. (See Pattern 8.)

B Jog. You are going to jog just a half circle and then change direction, so keep things relatively collected especially as you are headed toward cone C. (See Pattern 6.)

C Lope right lead. Your horse needs to be straightened and positioned just as you are finishing up your left half circle. So just as you approach the "kiss," or intersection, of the 8, straighten him and shift his weight to the left. Then apply the lope right lead aids. Don't get lost here. You are turning right and heading to cone D, not finishing up the circle you were on. (See Patterns 4 and 19.)

D Jog. Try to match the lope half of this lower circle in size and shape. (See Pattern 13.)

C Lope left lead. Same advice in reverse applies here as in the previous jog lope depart. Be sure your horse is straight for the depart. (See Patterns 4 and 19.)

B Stop. (See Pattern 5.)

Back 4 steps. (See Pattern 7.)

Find a place on the rail.

TIP TRANSITIONS

You have seven transitions to master and display in this pattern. A transition is a shifting upward or downward in the horse's gaits. A transition should be so smooth that the horse appears to blend or melt into the next gait. For a transition to be seamless, a horse must be prepared properly. If you surprise your horse with a sudden request, he might obey but in poor, stiff form. It is understandable why some transitions appear abrupt in a Horsemanship class because riders are trying to "hit the marks," that is, perform what is asked, exactly at the spot indicated on the pattern. It takes lots of practice to be accurate and smooth at the same time.

Transitions are a balance between your driving aids (seat and legs) and your restraining aids (upper body and hands).

PATTERN 18

C

B

A

Without stirrups:

A Jog

B Lope left lead circle

C Stop

Back 4 steps

Join new lineup

Pattern Help

Ride the entire pattern with your feet out of the stirrups.

A Jog. This is a fairly fast-moving pattern suitable for a big class. The judge will appreciate your being ready to go when it is your turn. Move up out of the lineup and have your horse's ears ready to go at the cone when the judge looks your way.

Riding without stirrups should be just like riding with stirrups: Your leg position should be the same. To jog, you push both seat bones forward, squeeze with both legs, and restrain the horse slightly with the bridle so that he doesn't jog too fast. Don't be tempted to grip with your legs as you jog, as this will make your horse jog faster and push you up out of the saddle, making it harder for you to sit securely. The best practice for riding without stirrups is to ride bareback, but you also need to practice riding in your saddle with your feet out of the stirrups. (See Pattern 9.)

B Lope left lead. When you are almost to cone B, you'd better get your horse in position for the lope depart; that is, shift his weight off to the right. Then lope left while his body is still straight. Then turn left. (See Patterns 4 and 19.)

Lope circle. There is no cone to indicate the size of the circle you are to lope. However, you should not go over 50 feet (15.3 m) in diameter as you would have to lope over a dozen strides, which might take too much time, especially if your horse is a slow loper. If the judge is standing about where you think you are going to make your circle, don't ever lope behind the judge. For one thing, the judge is probably standing there to indicate to you (in a subtle way) not to make the circle larger than that. Also, if you lope behind the judge, she will not be able to see you. Most important, it is dangerous for the judge to be used as a cone! (See Patterns 2 and 18.)

C Stop. (See Pattern 5.)

Back 4 steps. (See Pattern 7.)

Join the new lineup.

TIP ESTIMATING CIRCLE SIZE

For making a 50-foot (15.3 m) diameter circle at home, get five cones. Place one cone where you want the center of your circle. Then pace 5 strides in one direction and place a cone. Go back to the center cone and pace 5 strides in the opposite direction and place another cone. Then repeat, making a line that is perpendicular to the first diameter line you created. You will end up with four cones equally spaced around the perimeter of a medium-sized circle (about 50 feet [15.3 m] in diameter) and one cone at the center of the circle.

Walk to cone A

A Lope right lead

B Stop

   90-degree turn on
      hindquarters to the right

   Lope left lead circle

B Jog 2 strides

   Lope right lead

A Stop

   Back 4 steps

   Find a place on rail

Pattern Help

Walk to cone A. As your horse's ears are approaching cone A, apply pre-lope positioning aids to shift his weight to the left. (See Pattern 8.)

A With the marker on your left side, lope right lead. Immediately after the positioning aids, apply the lope right lead aids. You won't be loping a country mile, so keep your horse collected yet energetic. Think "slightly past the cone" so that you don't start sending body language signals to your horse too early for the stop. (See Pattern 12.)

B Stop. (See Pattern 5.)

90-degree turn on the hindquarters to the right. The pattern calls for a 90-degree turn, not a pivot, so technically the judge wants a walk-around turn on the hindquarters. Actually, it will be a little bit bigger than a 90-degree — about 110 degrees — in order to get you lined up to start the circle properly. If you perform a 90-degree turn, that's okay, too. It will just push the circle down to the end of the arena a little more. This is not a big deal. (See Tip at right.)

Lope left lead. After a turn to the right, a lope left lead comes pretty naturally because the horse is already in position after the turn and all you have to do is apply the lope aids. (See Patterns 4 and 22.)

Lope a circle. This is a big circle and intended to be *loped!* If your horse does a 4-beat, lazy, impure gait, it will take forever to get around this big circle. And the longer the judge has to wait, the more time there is to write down comments of the kind you don't want. (See Patterns 2 and 18.)

B Jog 2 strides. Make a straight line parallel to your entry line. Begin at least 1 lope stride before the jog. Since the jog is a 2-beat gait, 2 strides are 4 beats. The diagonal pair in lope left lead is left hind/right front. When the horse breaks down from the lope, the left hind and right front will be the first diagonal pair to land for the jog. If that diagonal pair is beat 1, beat 4 is right hind and left front. Since the left hind is the initiator of the lope right lead, the horse has to lope after beat 4 of the jog. This means you have to position your horse during beat 3 of the jog and give the lope aids during beat 4. (See Pattern 13.)

Lope right lead. This a short trip, so be sure you have your horse collected. (See Patterns 4 and 19.)

A Stop. The cone is on your left side. Ideally, stop with your horse's forehand right at the cone. (See Pattern 5.)

Back 4 steps. (See Pattern 7.)

Find a place on the rail.

TIP 90-DEGREE TURN ON THE HINDQUARTERS RIGHT

From a halt, keep the horse's body straight, but flex his head at the throatlatch slightly to the right. If you overbend the horse, he will likely step his hindquarters to the left as you turn.

- Position your right leg at the cinch, weight your right seat bone, and keep your right shoulder back.
- Rotate your left shoulder forward as you turn.
- Neck rein on the left side of the horse's neck, keeping horse straight in front and weight settled to the rear.
- Use an active left leg to turn the forehand to the right and to prevent a sideways step to the left by the hindquarters.

A Jog

B Turn left

C Lope left lead circle

C Simple change through
2 strides of jog

E Turn right

F Stop

Back 4 steps

Walk

Join new lineup

Pattern Help

A Jog. (See Pattern 9.)

B Turn left. (See Patterns 3, 6, and 16.)

C Lope left lead. (See Patterns 4 and 19.)

Lope circle. This pattern includes a cone to denote the size of the circle; the circle is to be made *inside* the cone. The circle is relatively small, about 30 feet (9.2 m) in diameter. This means it has a 94-foot (28.7-m) circumference. You should be able to fit about 9 strides at the lope in this small circle. This requires that you be right on the money on your lope depart so that you don't lose any footage there by jogging past cone C. Also, your horse will have to be collected and quite supple in his bending and solid in his neck reining, as this is not a circle for lumbering around. (See Patterns 2 and 18.)

C Simple change through 2 strides of jog. (See Pattern 19 for the same sequence in a different shape pattern.)

E Turn right. (See Pattern 15.)

F Stop. (See Pattern 5.)

Back 4 steps. (See Pattern 7.)

Walk.

Join the new lineup.

TIP CONES

Cones can help you learn how to make circles round, how to make straight lines straight, and how to determine lengths and sizes of maneuvers. They can give you goals for prompt, specific transitions. Practice heading directly at cones for those patterns that want you to aim at the center of a cone. Some judges want an exhibitor to perform exactly at a cone; other judges are more concerned with a smooth transition or maneuver, not absolute precision on the spot. Since you do not know which judges emphasize what, you will need to excel in both areas.

Be sure to also practice riding by cones that are close to your left and rights sides without stepping on them. You will need to try this a few times to gauge how close you can get to a cone without your horse stepping on it. At the show, be sure not to look down at cones, especially when stopping.

Especially in a pattern that calls for a halt and a 180- or 360-degree turn, you will need to know how much room to allow for the turn. It is a case of being the optimum distance. If you stop very short of the cone to be sure you have enough room, it shows that you haven't practiced enough to be confident on your distances. If you stop too close and hit the cone, you will receive a lower score. Whenever possible, ride on a track about 6 feet (1.8 m) from the cones, and stop at least that far away for performing a hindquarter or forehand turn.

A Jog

B Turn left

Walk

X Lope left lead circle

X Simple change through 2 steps of walk

X Lope right lead circle

X Stop

Dismount and mount

Walk

Return to lineup

B ⊙   ⊙ **A**

D ⊙   ⊙ **C**

Pattern Help

A Jog. (See Pattern 9.)

B Turn left. (See Patterns 3, 6, and 16.)

Just before X, walk. X is an imaginary spot. Walk about 3 feet (0.9 m) in front of X, just enough to establish the walk before the lope depart. The momentum of the jog will still be in your horse's mind and body. If you walk longer than a few strides, the loss of momentum will make the depart more difficult. (See Pattern 12.)

X Lope left lead. X is an imaginary spot. (See Patterns 4 and 19.)

Lope circle. This circle is to be ridden inside the cone. It's a medium circle, about 50 feet (15.3 m) in diameter, and requires about 15 lope strides. (See Patterns 2 and 18.)

X Simple change through 2 steps of walk. This should come fairly easily because your horse is in position, he still has the momentum, and your timing is impeccable! (See Pattern 16.)

X Lope right lead circle. (See Patterns 2 and 18.)

X Stop. (See Pattern 5.)

Dismount and mount. To dismount, remove your right foot from the stirrup; place your left hand, holding the reins, in front of the horse's withers, with your right hand on the horn or off swell; and tilt your upper body slightly forward as you swing your right leg over the horse's back. Step down close to the horse, facing his side or forward.

After dismount, it is correct to draw the reins over the horse's head and stand next to the horse facing forward. However, in the interest of time, the judge may want you to remount immediately without drawing the reins over the horse's head.

To mount, take up the reins in your left hand and place that hand in front of the withers. Face the horse's hindquarters. Grasp the near stirrup with your right hand, turn it toward you and insert your left foot in the stirrup. Turn the toe of your boot into the cinch so that you won't press into the horse's skin as you mount. Use your right hand to grasp either the horn or off swell. If you try to pull yourself up by the cantle, you will pull the saddle off to the near side. Step up or bounce once or twice on your right foot. Rise and swing your right leg over the horse's back and mount. Lower yourself softly into the saddle. Find the right stirrup by feel with your boot, not by looking for it.

Walk.

Return to the lineup.

Note: There is no back in this pattern, so the judge will ask for it in the lineup or on the rail. (See Pattern 39.)

TIP FIGURE 8

Ideally, the two sides of a figure 8 should be equal in size and round, except for the place where the circles touch. At the center of the figure 8, where the lead changes take place, the horse's body should be straight for 1 stride before and 1 stride after the lead change. This requires collection. Don't ride a lazy figure 8 where the circles are not round where they touch but instead have a squashed-down X in the center with long diagonals. Typically this results in a less-collected change (a front foot first or hind foot first change rather than a simultaneous change) and destroys the shape of the circles.

A Lope left lead

B Turn left

Simple change through
2 strides of jog

C Stop

Back 4 steps

Walk

Return to lineup

B

A

C

Pattern Help

A Lope left lead. (See Tip at right.)

B Turn left. (See Pattern 15.)

After the corner, simple change through 2 strides of jog to right lead. Be sure you wait until your horse is straight before you ask for the downward transition to the jog. (See Pattern 16.)

C Stop. (See Pattern 5.)

Back 4 steps. (See Pattern 7.)

Walk.

Return to the lineup.

TIP HALT TO LOPE

Everything you have learned about positioning aids and lope aids from the walk and jog apply here with modifications. When you ask a horse to lope from a standstill, you start with the horse standing with his four legs squarely underneath him.

When it is time to lope, you have to position him just like when he is moving at the walk or jog. When he is moving, it is not so noticeable that he shifts slightly over to his right before left lead aids are applied. But when he is at a standstill, it will be more noticeable that he shifts over to the right just before the depart. His body is straight, yet you shift his weight over to the right just a fraction of a second before you apply the lope left lead aids. You'll be driving deeper with your right seat bone as you push his right hind leg deep under his body, reaching forward.

If you push just your horse's hindquarters over to the right so that he is standing on a diagonal line, he will lope crooked, like a crab. This is very undesirable. His body must be straight. You need to move his shoulder over as well as his hindquarters.

Don't be tempted to lean your upper body forward in an attempt to help "jump-start" him. This just squashes your horse out behind you. And don't rock or pump your upper body to try to get him started. At home you will need to work on providing the extra incentive that is necessary to get a lope from a halt through your aids while at the same time maintaining proper position.

A good exercise is lope-walk-lope-halt-lope with very little time in between transitions. You can practice this in one direction in the arena, asking for the same lead each time. Then reverse and practice it in the opposite direction on the other lead. Then practice on a straight line and alternate which leads you request to prevent your horse from anticipating.

A Walk 2 strides

Lope left lead

B Turn left

X Simple change through
    2 steps of walk

Lope circle

X Simple change through
    2 strides of jog

Lope circle

X Stop

Jog

Return to lineup

B   **A**

D   **C**

Pattern Help

A Walk 2 strides. That is 8 beats, which require about 11 feet (3.4 m). (See Pattern 8.)

Lope left lead. (See Pattern 12.)

B Turn left. (See Pattern 15.)

X Simple change through 2 steps of walk to right lead. With 2 steps of walk, this change should occur naturally. Try to have your lope depart occur midway between cones C and D. Use your peripheral vision to note where the cones are; do not look from side to side as though you are going to cross the street. (See Pattern 16.)

Lope circle to the right. These medium-sized circles are to be ridden inside the cones. You'll fit about 10 strides of lope here if this is about a 35-foot (10.7-m) diameter circle. (See Patterns 2 and 18.)

X Simple change through 2 strides of jog to left lead. (See Pattern 16.)

Lope circle to the left. (See Patterns 2 and 18.)

X Stop. (See Pattern 5.)

Jog. (See Pattern 9.)

Return to the lineup. Be sure to break down to a walk as you approach the line, so you don't startle any horses in the lineup. You don't want to cause any problems for your fellow exhibitors.

Note: There is no back in this pattern, so the judge will ask for it in the lineup or on the group rail. (See Pattern 39.)

TIP GOOD HORSEMANSHIP

Even though competition is healthy and helps you set goals, don't let it make you lose sight of good horsemanship and sportsmanship. Never treat your horse with disrespect. If he makes a mistake, 9 times out of 10 it is because you made a mistake or didn't prepare him properly. That's why it makes no sense to punish him if he makes an error.

This is a relatively easy pattern for an intermediate rider, so the tendency is to take it easy — no problem! But if you do have a problem, you can almost always be sure it was pilot error or lack of sufficient training, *not* the fault of your horse. First, look to yourself to improve. Always. *Never* be abusive of your horse if he makes a mistake. He will lose his trust in you, and your pattern work will suffer in the future.

PATTERN 24

A Jog 2 strides

Extend the jog

B Walk

C Lope left lead circle

D Simple change through 2 steps of walk

E Stop

Back 6 steps

Walk

Return to lineup

Pattern Help

A Jog 2 strides. This means 4 beats and requires about 16 feet (4.9 m) of your straight line between cones A and B. It looks like you'll have plenty of room to exhibit your extended jog. (See Pattern 9.)

Extend the jog. Sit the extended jog; do not post. (See Tip at right.) Here is something the pattern doesn't tell you. After the extended jog, a good rider returns to a regular jog before performing any other transitions. So, as you near cone B, diminish your driving aids and gather your horse up to balance him for at least one stride before cone B.

B Walk. This should be on a nice light contact. You shouldn't have to hold your horse down into a walk. (See Patterns 5 and 8.)

C Lope left lead. (See Pattern 12.)

Lope circle. (See Patterns 2 and 18.)

D Simple change through 2 steps of walk to right lead. (See Pattern 16.)

E Stop. (See Pattern 5.)

Back 6 steps. (See Patterns 7, 42, and 50.)

Walk and return to the lineup.

TIP EXTENDED JOG

The extended jog is an increase in stride length without an increase in rhythm. The legs don't move quicker, but the legs do reach farther, resulting in a longer, more ground-covering stride. The extended jog should be smooth. You sit the extended jog; do not post.

To extend the jog, tilt your pelvis back, which deepens your seat bones and pushes them forward in the saddle. Drive forward with your seat and legs. This sends the horse's hind legs deeper under his belly and results in a longer stride. When you tilt your pelvis back (which feels like the push off on a swing), be sure you don't lean your upper body back.

You want to give the horse a little "headroom" into which he can extend, so move your reining hand forward inviting him to reach forward with his neck as well. A judge will be looking for an increase in the length of the horse's stride without a quickening of the tempo of his jog. Display some courage and show the judge a detectable change!

PATTERN 25

E   D   B   A

C

A Extended jog

B Jog

C Lope left lead

D Simple change through
2 steps of walk

E Stop

Back 4 steps

Walk

Join new lineup

PATTERN HELP

A Extended jog. To exhibit an extended jog at cone A, I suggest you jog right out of the lineup and then extend the jog when you get to cone A. You don't have a whole lot of room between cones A and B to show an extension, so you'd better hit the mark right at cone A. You don't need to wind down from the extended jog to a jog before cone B because a regular jog is what is called for there, so you can show the extended jog on the entire cone A-B line. (See Patterns 9 and 22.)

B Jog. You need to power down, collect, and bend all at once. Note that C is not a cone but rather an invisible marker. It might be a spot of lime in the arena dirt or it might just be an imaginary mark. You might have some leeway here as far as circle size.

C Lope left lead. Keep the left bend from the jog half circle, but shift the horse up onto the outside rein just before you ask for the left lead. It would be an oddity for a horse to take the incorrect lead when he has already worked half of a circle. After you return to cone B, straighten your horse as quickly as you can because you only have 1 to 2 strides of lope before you walk. (See Patterns 4 and 19.)

D Simple change through 2 steps of walk to right lead. The straighter your horse is at the walk, the easier it will be to lope off on the right lead. I suggest your horse be walking when the tips of his ears hit cone D. Otherwise you might find yourself running out of room for your right lead lope. You should be able to strike off and fit 3 strides of lope between cones D and E. (See Pattern 16.)

If you did not quite make cone D as planned and find yourself running short of room, don't throw away the rest of the pattern. Rather than losing points on your strike off, the stop, and the back because you feel cramped and nervous, just relax and plan to overshoot cone E by a stride or two so you get a nice stop and back. It's not the end of the world. It's just a simple choice. And I suggest you always opt for smoothness, finesse, and consideration for your horse. Those are signs of true horsemanship.

E Stop. (See Pattern 5.)

Back 4 steps. (See Pattern 7.)

Walk. (See Patterns 5 and 8.)

Join the new lineup.

TIP | **WORKING AWAY FROM THE GROUP**

Even at the intermediate level, some riders lack sufficient control of their mounts to guide them in individual maneuvers away from the rest of the lineup. This results in a pattern becoming lopsided as the horse performs willingly toward the lineup but reluctantly away from it. Because the horse is a social animal, he desires companionship with others, especially during times of stress. If the horse is unsure of his rider or the situation, he will want to return to the safety of the rest of the horses in the class. The rider who has developed a confident horse has little problem asking him to work independently. When you are "breaking in" a new or young horse to showing, be sure you spend plenty of time at home setting up show ring situations so that your horse learns the routine and doesn't become a "groupie" or a "rail bird."

A Jog

B Stop

Back 4 steps

Lope left lead

C Walk

D Lope right lead

E Jog

F Walk

Exit gate

PATTERN HELP

This pattern has no cones. It is a free-form pattern that will test your ability to approximate the written pattern. When a judge uses a pattern like this, she is more likely interested in forward movement and good shapes. She'll expect absolutely silky-smooth transitions because she's letting you pick the moment they occur. Think of the pattern as straight lines down the long side, and along the short end, followed by two half circles and straight work on the diagonal. Piece it together, and draw the picture in your mind.

A Jog. Jog about halfway down the long side of the arena. (See Pattern 9.)

B Stop. It is great to be able to stop when you feel things are right rather than having to stop simply because a pesky orange cone happens to be there! Take advantage of this freedom, and gather your horse for a smooth, square stop. (See Pattern 3.)

Back 4 steps. (See Pattern 7.)

Lope left lead. This is a new one, a lope from a back. Your lope should be very cadenced, forward and lively yet collected. Your horse should cover some ground yet be in top form. Lope around the end of the arena and when you are on the second corner of the short end, make a half circle back toward the opposite long side. (See Tip at right and Patterns 4, 22, 30, and 35.)

C Walk. As soon as you are straight, walk. The walk, too, should be very forward, and you've been given plenty of room — about 10 strides — to demonstrate that the horse can walk.

If your horse is a dawdler, you'll be so anxious for the lope that you might rush. Work on developing a forward walk with your horse at home. (See Pattern 10.)

D Lope right lead. Lope at about the center line of the arena. As soon as you have loped, make a half circle turn to the right and head across the arena's diagonal. (See Patterns 10 and 12.)

E Jog. Jog about 8 to 10 strides, looking straight ahead to the outgate. (See Pattern 13.)

F Walk. About 15 feet (4.6 m) before you hit the outgate, walk. (See Pattern 12.)

Exit the gate.

TIP BACK TO LOPE

This is a transition from a diagonal gait in reverse to a forward gait that has a diagonal pair. Since you want to lope left lead after the back, the diagonal pair for that lead is the left hind and right front. When those legs have landed at the end of your back, it is time to cue for the lope left lead. The right hind will be the first leg to drive off in the lope. The timing is crucial. And what you do will depend on which diagonal your horse started to back with.

When you are in the third step of the back, if the diagonal pair that is landing is the right hind and left front, you are in good shape. All you do is decrease the intensity of your back aids during the fourth step. At the same time, you rev up your forward driving lope aids and apply them just as the horse rocks his weight back on the right hind for the push off.

D

C

B

A

A Back to cone B

B 180-degree turn on the
      hindquarters to the left

Lope left lead

C Jog

D Stop square

Stand 3 seconds

Walk

Find a place on rail

Pattern Help

A Back to cone B. If the cones are set about 10 feet (3.1 m) apart, this will require you to back about 2 strides, or 4 beats. The critical aspect of the beginning of this pattern, however, is how close you can be to the cones and still perform the 180-degree turn to the left. The horse in the drawing would crunch the cone during the turn — and cone crunching is not good. You need to be at least 5 feet (1.5 m) from the cone so that when you turn, your horse's front feet don't run into the cone. (See Patterns 30 and 35.)

B 180-degree turn on the hindquarters to the left. Start the turn when your horse's left hind leg is set well under his body as this will be the pivot point of the turn. If you start with his left hind leg camped way out behind, you will get a very discombobulated turn. He'll either have to step forward or back in a hurry, or he might pivot on his outside hind leg. Keep your horse's body straight, with just slight left flexion, and pilot him around with a right neck rein and active right leg. Weight your left seat bone and bring your right shoulder forward, but keep your right leg ready to contain his hindquarter so that it doesn't step to the right.

You *don't* want a turn on the center, which is also called "swapping ends" and occurs when a horse swivels on his middle, stepping left with his forehand and right with his hindquarters. Avoid this. It is not a judge pleaser.

Lope left lead. A lope left lead from a left hindquarter turn can flow smoothly if the turn was active. If the turn was halting, this will not be the easiest setup and requires some thought and practice. (See Tip at right and Patterns 4 and 22.)

C Jog. (See Pattern 13.)

D Stop square. A square stop is one where the horse's body is directly on the line of the pattern. His hind legs are directly behind his front legs, not offset to the left or right. His cannon bones are vertical. This puts his front legs next to each other and directly below his shoulders, not propped in front or angled behind. His hind legs are next to each other, and the cannons are positioned directly below his hocks or set just a bit under, but not camped out or angled excessively under. The square stop is a balanced, collected, planned stop, which shows great conditioning and training. (See Pattern 3.)

Stand 3 seconds. (See Pattern 1.)

Walk. (See Patterns 5 and 8.)

Find a place on the rail.

TIP | **LEFT HINDQUARTER TURN TO LOPE LEFT LEAD**

Try to make this all one movement so the maneuver will flow. You must be very aware of your horse's body position to make this happen. What you need to do is:

- Keep your horse's body straight during the turn.

- As you finish the 180-degree turn on the line, be sure your horse's weight is still balanced on the right side of his body (pre-lope positioning aids).

- Apply aids for lope left lead.

  A well-trained horse will accept this progression fine, but an inexperienced, less-confident horse might be confused. That's why you need to properly prepare your horse at home with lots of practice. Be careful not to let the horse's weight fall on his forehand or to the left as you finish the turn. He needs to be "light" on his left forehand in order to strike off on the left lead.

A Walk

B Jog

C Lope left lead

D Lope circle

E Stop

180-degree turn on the
hindquarters to the right

Lope right lead

F Stop

Back 4 steps

Walk

Return to lineup

C

B

A

D

E

F

Pattern Help

A Walk. You have room for about 2 strides here. (See Pattern 8.)

B Jog. You'll be able to jog 4 to 6 strides before you prepare for the lope. (See Pattern 6.)

C Lope left lead. Position and lope your horse while he is still straight, then turn at C. (See Patterns 4 and 19.)

D Lope circle. This is a tiny circle for a lope. If it is 20 feet (6.1 m) in diameter, you'll be lucky to fit 6 strides of lope in it, so your horse must be very collected. If you are riding a large horse or a strung-out horse, you are going to have to make the circle larger. Remember, though, that the intent is a small circle that does not cross the line that goes to cone F. (See Patterns 12 and 18.)

E Stop. (See Pattern 5.)

180-degree turn on the hindquarters to the right. Start the turn when your horse's right hind leg (pivot point) is set well under his body for the turn. Keep your horse's body straight with just slight right flexion, and pilot him around with a left neck rein. Weight your right seat bone and bring your left shoulder forward, but keep your left leg ready to contain his hindquarter so that it doesn't step to the left.

Lope right lead. Right hindquarter turn to lope right lead can flow well with promptness and balance. Be careful not to let your horse "stall" in the turn or fall on his forehand. You must be very aware of your horse's body position to make this happen. What you need to do is:

★ Keep your horse's body straight during the turn.

★ As you are finishing the 180-degree turn, be sure your horse's weight is still balanced on the left side of his body (pre-lope positioning aids).

★ Apply aids for lope right lead.

F Stop. (See Pattern 5.)

Back 4 steps. (See Pattern 7.)

Walk.

Return to the lineup.

TIP | LEADS

Since Horsemanship and Equitation classes judge the rider, not the horse, a horse that is not perfectly trained can be used. Such a horse might occasionally strike off on the incorrect lead. If the rider immediately recognizes the incorrect lead and brings the horse back down to a walk or jog and strikes off on the correct lead, it shows the judge that the rider knows the difference between leads and knows how to correct it. Never get angry at a horse when he takes the incorrect lead in a show. If you show impatience or loss of temper, even if you do correct the lead problem, you will not get good marks from the judge. More importantly, aggressive behavior on your part will undermine your horse's confidence.

A Walk

B Sidepass to cone C

C Lope left lead

E Stop

180-degree turn on the
hindquarters to the right

Lope right lead

D Jog

C Stop

Back 4 steps

Pattern Help

A Walk. (See Pattern 8.)

B Sidepass to cone C. (See Tip below.)

C Lope left lead. This is a gift to counterbalance what comes later in this pattern. Here you get a great setup. The sidepass to lope is a wonderful at-home training exercise and here you've been served it in a perfect combination: sidepass right to lope left lead. What this does is set your horse up perfectly for a lope depart. The sidepass keeps his body straight and weights his right side so that he is positioned for the application of the lope left lead aids. (See Patterns 4 and 22.)

E Stop. (See Pattern 5.)

180-degree turn on the hindquarters to the right. (See Pattern 28.)

Lope right lead. This is the tricky combination described earlier. (See Pattern 28.)

D Jog. (See Pattern 13.)

C Stop. (See Pattern 7.)

Back 4 steps.

TIP SIDEPASS

You can ride a sidepass with your horse straight (best in this situation), counter-flexed (easiest for first training a horse), or flexed into the direction of the sidepass (most difficult). In all cases, the seat and leg aids and footfall patterns are the same. Only the rein aids are different.

For a sidepass to the right, the footfall sequence is the same as the 4 beat walk; the action is as follows:

1. Left hind crosses over in front of the right hind.
2. Left front crosses over in front of the right front.
3. Right hind uncrosses from behind the left hind and steps to the right.
4. Right front uncrosses from behind the left front and steps to the right.

Steps 2 and 3 happen almost in unison, allowing the horse to retain his balance.

To sidepass right:

- Weight your left seat bone.
- Apply your left leg at or behind the cinch and use it in rhythm with the lifting of the left hind leg; this is a sideways driving aid.
- Keep your right leg on the horse, but very lightly; do not take your leg off the horse and allow daylight between your leg and the horse's side.
- Lay the left neck rein on the horse's neck, but keep the horse's neck straight.

E   D   C   B   A

A Back

B 180-degree turn on the
       hindquarters to the right

       Lope right lead

C Simple change through
       1 stride of walk

       Lope circle

       Jog

D Extended jog

E Stop

Pattern Help

When a pattern starts with a back, you will move along in the lineup until it is your time to begin. You have the option of either facing forward until the judge gives you the nod to begin and then getting into position (using a combination of either a turn on the hindquarters or forehand with a sidepass) or of being in position when he gives you the nod. If you are facing backward, it will be awkward to twist around to watch the judge, so it's usually better to stay facing forward and make your orientation switch smoothly just before you start your pattern.

A Back. (See Pattern 7.)

B 180-degree turn on the hindquarters to the right. (See Pattern 28.)

   Lope right lead. (For help and sympathy, see Pattern 28.)

C Simple change through 1 stride of walk. (See Pattern 16.)

   Lope left lead. (See Pattern 4.)

   Lope circle. (See Patterns 2 and 18.)

   Close circle, then jog. (See Pattern 13.)

D Extended jog. In order to get a collected, square stop, you must bring your horse back to a normal jog for 1 stride before you stop. (See Pattern 24.)

E Stop. (See Pattern 3.)

TIP FINISHING THE BACK

When you need to perform another maneuver after a back, you don't want to finish the back with the horse's legs sprawled out behind him as this would make it difficult for you to organize the horse to perform the next maneuver. You can just hope things work out, but there's a much better chance of success if you plan and practice.

Decrease your back aids 1 step before you are finished backing. In this case, during the third step backward, diminish your aids so that your horse won't take a large step to finish the back. This will put you in a better position to prepare for your 180-degree turn. Because it is a turn to the right, finish the back when the horse's right hind leg (the pivot point of the turn) is well under him.

A Jog 3 strides

Lope left lead

B Turn left

C Stop

360-degree turn on the
hindquarters to the left

Walk

Return to lineup

B

A

C

PATTERN HELP

A Jog 3 strides. That is 6 beats and requires about 24 feet (7.3 m). (See Pattern 9.)

Lope left lead. (See Patterns 4 and 19.)

B Turn left. (See Pattern 15.)

C Stop. (See Pattern 5.)

360-degree turn on the hindquarters to the left. Give yourself at least 6 feet (1.8 m) for the turn. Be sure to settle after the turn before you walk off. (See Tip at right.)

Walk 2 to 3 strides. (See Patterns 5 and 8.)

Return to the lineup. Move up to a jog or lope to get out of the judge's line of vision.

Note: There is no back in this pattern, so the judge will ask for it in the lineup or on the rail. (See Pattern 39.)

TIP 360-DEGREE TURN TO THE LEFT

At home, train your horse this way. Walk him in a straight line, making sure his body is straight. Sit centered over your horse with slightly more weight on your left seat bone. Keep your eyes up and glance around as you turn. With your right neck rein and your right leg on his ribs, begin turning him into a small circle. Be sure your inside rein is fairly slack. As your horse begins to cross his right front leg over his left front leg, use a stronger right leg aid against his ribs and lay the right neck rein a little more strongly on his neck. Keep your left leg from pressing his ribs so that he knows he can move to the left. Continue in the very small circle until he is pivoting on his left hind leg. Be sure his body stays straight. If his head turns into the left too much, it will cause his hindquarters to swing off to the right. If he gets behind the bit or starts backing up or locking up, you will need to straighten your rein aid and drive him forward with both legs. At the show you will not be able to perform the pre-turn circle so eventually you will have to remove it, but keep the "idea" of a forward circle there as you perform your 360-degree turn on the hindquarters.

Walk to cone A

A Jog

B Stop

 360-degree turn on the
  hindquarters to the right

 Lope left lead

 Lope balloon to the left

B Jog 1 stride

 Lope right lead

C Stop

 Back 5 steps

 90-degree turn on the
  hindquarters to the left

 Walk

 Exit arena

Pattern Help

Walk to cone A.

A Jog. (See Pattern 9.)

B Stop. (See Pattern 3.)

360-degree turn on the hindquarters to the right. Settle the horse's weight slightly rearward onto the right hind leg (pivot point) without actually backing. Don't settle the weight too deeply or you will lose the forward motion of the turn. Keep your right leg passive at the cinch. Using a left neck rein, start turning the horse right with an active left leg at or behind the cinch. Your left shoulder should come slightly ahead of your right shoulder for the turn. As long as your horse's weight stays settled on his right hind pivot foot, you should have no problem with him stepping sideways (to the left) with his hindquarter. However, have your left leg ready to move behind the cinch to hold the hindquarters. Keep your horse's body straight and be sure he maintains the 4-beat walk time as he crosses left front over right front.

Lope left lead. (See Patterns 4 and 22.)

Lope balloon to the left. (See Pattern 8.)

B Jog 1 stride. (See Pattern 16.)

Lope right lead. (See Pattern 10.)

C Stop. (See Pattern 5.)

Back 5 steps. (See Pattern 7.)

90-degree turn on the hindquarters to the left. The pattern calls for a 90-degree walk-around turn on the hindquarters, not a pivot. From a halt, keep the horse's body straight but flex his head at the throatlatch slightly to the left. If you overbend the horse, he will likely step his hindquarters to the right as you turn.

★ Left leg at the cinch, weight your left seat bone, left shoulder back.

★ Right shoulder rotates forward as you turn.

★ Neck rein on the right side of the horse's neck, keeping horse straight in front and weight settled to the rear.

★ Right leg behind the cinch to prevent sideways step to the right.

Walk.

Exit arena.

TIP DEVELOPING FINESSE

It is time to polish your performance and develop finesse. When you were a novice horsemanship exhibitor, you might have over-cued your horse to ensure that he performed the prescribed maneuvers at the right spot. Rein cues given outside an imaginary 6-inch (15.2-cm) square box in the vicinity of the saddle horn will be noticed by the judge, and sweeping cues 12 inches (30.5 cm) or more to one side or another of the horse's neck will be heavily penalized. The goal at the end of the intermediate stage is to have invisible hand movements or operate rein cues in a 4-inch (10.2-cm) or smaller square box and to ride the horse primarily with your seat and legs. Gone are the days when you pull the bridle reins in an attempt to back. Now, you have established contact with the bit and you back the horse with leg cues. You no longer consider an exaggerated shift of your weight to initiate a lead depart since it creates an unbalanced situation for both you and your horse. If you wear spurs, you use them sparingly. You use subtle weight and leg cues for initiation of lope departs, hindquarter turns, neck reining, and backing.

Advanced Western Horsemanship Patterns

Advanced level riders use subtle aids to produce precise patterns. Advanced patterns include all of the maneuvers found in beginning and intermediate patterns plus flying lead changes, 360-degree turns on the hindquarters, pivots, spins, back and turn, counter-canter, and other maneuvers.

On the following page, you'll find four blank arenas where you can record patterns that you've ridden at shows.

TRAINING NOTES

COMPETITION GOALS

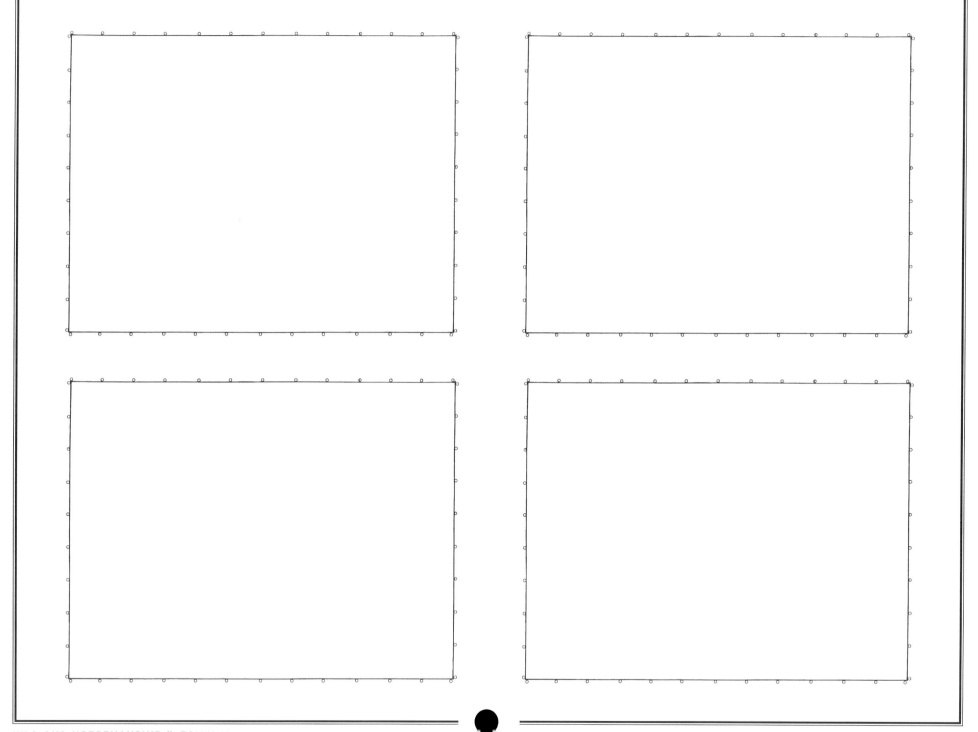

A Lope left lead

B Flying change

Lope right circle

B Jog

C Stop

Back 4 steps

360-degree turn to the right

Walk

Find a place on rail

PATTERN HELP

A Lope left lead. (See Patterns 4 and 22.)

B Flying change to right lead. (See Tip at right.) Be sure to make the change while your horse is straight. Then create the bend for the circle.

> **Lope right circle.** (See Patterns 2 and 18.)

B Jog. (See Pattern 13.)

C Stop. (See Pattern 3.)

> **Back 4 steps.** (See Pattern 7.)

> **360-degree turn to the right.** (See Pattern 32.)

> **Walk.** (See Patterns 5 and 8.)

> **Find a place on the rail.**

This pattern is designed to be very short for large classes.

TIP FLYING CHANGE TO RIGHT LEAD

A flying change consists of a three-point check, pre-positioning aids, and the lead change itself.

Three-Point Check. As you are preparing for a flying change from left to right, you need to check three things:

1. Be sure your horse is loping at a true 3-beat lope. If he is "4-beating," he won't have enough impulsion and his legs won't be in the right place at the right time for a change.
2. Be sure your horse's body is straight. It is much more difficult to get a clean, prompt lead change if your horse's spine is curved.
3. Be sure you feel contact with the horse through the reins. You should be able to further collect your horse by just moving your hand back 1 inch (2.5 cm). And if you move your hand forward 1 inch (2.5 cm), he should stretch forward.

Pre-positioning. Now, with your horse loping on the left lead, move your reining hand over to the left, which applies a right neck rein on the horse. You are shifting the horse's weight to his left side much like you do for a lope depart. At the same time, put your right leg on the horse to shift his weight left. When you are loping on the left lead, your left seat bone is more forward than your right seat bone. You can hold this pre-change position for 2 to 3 strides of lope at home if you want. At the show, you want to hone it down to 1 stride.

The Change. For the change, keep the horse straight and up on his left shoulder so that his right shoulder is "free" to change. Do this by maintaining contact and using a slight right neck rein.

- Relax the pressure of your right leg that is holding the horse to the left (this "invites" the horse to the right), and move your right seat bone forward.

- Apply your left leg behind the cinch to ask for the change just as you would for a lope depart.

A Jog

B Turn left

X Lope left lead circle

Flying change

Lope right lead circle

Stop

Back 4 steps

Walk

Return to lineup

B

A

PATTERN HELP

A Jog. Here's where you hope your horse has a good ground covering jog because this is about 15 to 20 strides of jog. If your horse takes forever to get to X, you will have to work on developing a more forward jog with your horse. (See Pattern 9.)

B Turn left. (See Patterns 3, 6, and 16.)

X Lope left lead. (See Patterns 4 and 19.)

Lope a circle to the left. This 40-foot (12.2 m) circle requires about 12 lope strides. (See Patterns 2 and 18.)

Flying change to right lead. (See Pattern 33.)

Lope a circle to the right. (See Patterns 2 and 18.)

Stop. (See Pattern 5.)

Back 4 steps. (See Pattern 7.)

Walk.

Return to the lineup. Pick up a jog or lope to get out of the judge's line of vision.

TIP WHEN TO ASK FOR A FLYING CHANGE

The best time to apply the actual aids for the change is when the horse's leading foreleg is landing. That gives the perfect window of opportunity to the initiating hind of the "new lead" to swap roles with the hind of the "old lead." The front legs change in the air and the flying change is complete.

A Lope left lead

Turn left

B Lope a small, slow circle

C Simple lead change
through 2 steps of walk

D Lope a large, fast circle

Jog

E Stop

Back 4 steps

360-degree turn on
the hindquarters
to the right

Walk

Return to lineup

A

B

C

D

E

PATTERN HELP

A Lope left lead. A lope from a standstill requires you to position your horse perfectly with his nose at cone A. Use your left leg at the cinch to hold him over to the right so that when you use your right leg behind the cinch to ask for the depart he strikes off on the correct lead and tracks a straight line. The lope must be fairly collected because you will only be loping about 40 feet (12.2 m) (4 strides) before you turn left. (See Pattern 22.)

Turn left. There isn't a cone to designate where you will make your turn. Aim at cone E at the end of the straightaway. When turning, don't cut across the corner on a diagonal or it will be difficult to get on the straight line. (See Pattern 15.)

B Lope a small, slow circle. Lope a small, slow circle to the left on the left lead. This circle should be about 20 to 30 feet (6.1–9.2 m) in diameter, which allows you only 6 to 7 strides, so the lope must be collected *and* slow at the beginning of the circle and all throughout. (See Patterns 2 and 18.)

C Simple lead change through 2 steps of walk. Just as you finish the circle and straighten your horse, drop to a walk for 2 steps and then strike off on the right lead. You're essentially going from left bend to straight at the same time you perform a downward transition. Then you perform an upward transition to lope at the same time you go from straight to right bend. Lope normal speed for the first stride of lope, which is straight, and for the first stride of the large circle. (See Pattern 16.)

D Lope a large, fast circle. This should be an extended lope or gallop in a 60-foot (18.3-m) (or larger) diameter circle to the right. Drop down to a normal lope for 1 stride before your transition to jog. (See Patterns 2 and 18.)

Jog. Jog when you return to the straight line. (See Pattern 13.)

E Stop. By the time you get to cone E, you should have reestablished a quiet rhythm and obtain a balanced, square stop. You need to be balanced on your six points of contact: two seat bones, two lower legs, and two reins in your hand. (See Pattern 3.)

Back 4 steps. Pause for just 1 second if necessary after the stop and begin backing. Since the pattern calls for 4 steps of back, be aware of the horse's movement. Often taking too many or not enough back steps can make a great difference in the placings. Since you will need to perform a turn to the right after the back, you want to be sure that your horse finishes the back with his legs square or with his right hind leg ahead of his left hind leg, but not the opposite. (See Pattern 7.)

360-degree turn on the hindquarters to the right. The required turn is not a spin, so you should perform a walk-around turn, controlled and precise, with the horse pivoting on his right hind leg. (See Pattern 32.)

Walk and return to the lineup. Leave the straight line of the pattern at a walk. After a few strides when you see the judge is looking at the next contestant, jog back to the lineup. (See Patterns 5 and 8.)

TIP SMILE

Without appearing artificial or losing your concentration, let a smile be part of your pattern. A smile shows confidence, takes some of the tension out of the exhibition, and is a nice treat for the judge and spectators.

PATTERN 36

A Walk 3 strides
 Jog
B Lope left lead
C Lope circle
D Flying change
 Lope circle
E Stop
 Back 5 steps
 Walk
 Return to lineup

B

A

C

D

E

PATTERN HELP

A Walk 3 strides. That's 12 steps, which take about 16 feet (4.9 m). (See Patterns 5 and 8.)

Then jog. You'll be able to fit in about 3 to 5 strides here. (See Pattern 6.)

B Lope left lead. (See Patterns 4 and 19.)

Turn. (See Pattern 15.)

C Lope circle to the left. This is a medium-sized circle that should allow 8 to 10 lope strides. (See Patterns 2 and 18.)

D Flying change to right lead. Be sure you and your horse are straight before, during, and after the change. (See Pattern 33.)

Lope circle to the right. Initiate right bend *after* the flying change. (See Patterns 2 and 18.)

E Stop. (See Pattern 5.)

Back 5 steps. (See Pattern 7.)

Walk.

Return to the lineup.

TIP FORWARD MOVEMENT, FORWARD TRANSITIONS

Well-trained Horsemanship horses, especially once they get to the advanced level, can tend to mellow out so much that they lose their forward impulsion. They have seen just about every kind of show ring and pattern imaginable. They have performed so many transitions that they start to function robotically. It is no wonder, then, that the zip, forward pizzazz, energy, and gusto go out of their performance. Though it is nice to see a quiet, calm performance, if it starts to become lifeless and robotic, then it seems as though the rider isn't really doing anything anymore; the horse is just on automatic pilot. This makes it more difficult for the judge to assess the rider's ability.

To prevent burnout in your horse and to restore forward movement, try some of the following:

- Do some trail riding.
- Gallop through a pasture.
- Switch to English Equitation.
- At home, practice patterns with lots of extended jog, extended lope, and gallop.
- Incorporate a lot of posting jog work in your at-home routines.

B

A

C

D

A Walk

B Lope left lead

C Flying change

Lope right circle

C Jog

B Stop

Back 4 steps

360-degree turn on the
hindquarters to the left

Find a place on rail

Pattern Help

A Walk. Be sure you do some trail riding with your horse. It's the best for developing a rein-swinging walk, which you will want here. With 15 to 20 strides of walk, you will want your horse to walk out. (See Pattern 8.)

B Lope left lead. The cones are set up for generous medium-sized circles to give you plenty of room for what is coming. (See Patterns 2, 12, and 18.)

C Flying change to right lead. The flying change is called to take place on the side of cone C that is closer to cone B. Be sure you pay attention to a detail like this. If you make the error of performing the change below cone C, then you will either have a very tight circle inside cone D or you will have to make a second error, which would be to ride your second circle below cone D. Right after the flying change, you will have to change from left to right bend. (See Pattern 33.)

Lope right circle. You can catch your breath a minute here as you lope a complete circle to the right. (See Patterns 2 and 18.)

C Jog. Don't let your horse fall on his forehand on the downward transition to jog, and be sure to keep the second half of the upper circle the same size as the first half was. (See Pattern 13.)

B Stop. (See Pattern 3.)

Back 4 steps. (See Pattern 7.)

360-degree turn on the hindquarters to the left. Settle your horse's weight to the left hind leg. Don't back. Weight your left seat bone, and keep your left leg passive at the cinch. Use a right neck rein and an active right leg to turn the horse. Your right shoulder will be slightly ahead of your left shoulder in the turn. Have your right leg ready to move behind the cinch to hold the hindquarters if necessary. Keep your horse's body straight, and be sure he maintains the 4-beat walk time as he crosses left front over right front. This is where the pattern ends, so you can walk a few steps and then lope out of the way.

Find a place on the rail.

TIP PREPARATION

More than 95 percent of your horse time will be spent caring for your horse, perfecting your riding and your horse's training, and traveling to the show. Since less than 5 percent of your time will be in the show ring, you must enjoy the preparation as much or more than the show ring participation.

If you are one of those horse owners who loves trimming a mane to perfection, giving your horse a good rubdown with plenty of elbow grease, cleaning a hoof until is looks picture perfect, exercising your horse every day to keep him fit and healthy, and tending to tack so that it is always in safe working condition and show-ring ready, then you will likely have a long and successful show-ring career.

PATTERN 38

A Walk 2 strides
   Lope left lead
B Turn left
X Lope circle to the left
   Flying change
   Lope circle to the right
   Stop
   Jog
   Return to lineup

Pattern Help

A Walk 2 strides. Move up to cone A as soon as the previous rider starts jogging. (See Patterns 5, 8, and 44.)

Lope left lead. (See Pattern 12.)

B Turn left. (See Pattern 15.)

X Lope circle to the left. These circles should not cramp your style, but be sure to stay inside the cones. (See Patterns 2 and 18.)

Flying change. X is an imaginary point. Be sure you are straight going into, through, and out of X. (See Pattern 33.)

Lope circle to the right. After the change, create right bend. (See Patterns 2 and 18.)

Stop. Pause for 1 to 2 seconds. (See Pattern 5.)

Jog. (See Pattern 9.)

Return to the lineup.

Note: There is no back in this pattern, so the judge will ask for it in the lineup or on the rail. (See Pattern 39.)

TIP PREVENTING ANTICIPATION

Most patterns call for a back after a stop. When a judge calls for a pattern without a back, she wants to see if you have schooled your horse to prevent anticipation. If you can stop and pause 1 to 2 seconds with your horse standing perfectly still, it shows that you have prepared your horse at home. It is nice for exhibitors to have a great variety in patterns because it helps them keep their horses from getting stale. To further keep your horse fresh, practice stops at home where you just stop square and stand, or lope through the place where your horse anticipates stopping, or stop and lope off again immediately.

A Jog 4 steps

Lope left lead

B Turn left

Flying change

C Stop

360-degree turn on the
hindquarters to the right

Walk

Return to lineup

B

A

C

Pattern Help

A Jog 4 steps. Four steps are equal to 2 strides, which requires about 16 feet (4.9 m). Watch your horse's shoulders by glancing down without lowering your head. Note which shoulder reaches forward first from the standstill. If it is the left, then the next time it reaches forward, it will be the third step. You will be applying pre-lope positioning aids during the third and fourth steps. (See Patterns 9 and 19.)

Lope left lead. (See Patterns 4 and 19.)

B Turn left. (See Pattern 15.)

Just after the corner, flying change to right lead. (See Pattern 33.)

C Stop. (See Pattern 5.)

360-degree turn on the hindquarters to the right. (See Pattern 32.)

Walk.

Return to the lineup.

Note: There is no back in this pattern, so the judge will ask for it in the lineup or on the rail. (See Tip at right.)

TIP WHEN BACKING IS NOT IN THE PATTERN

When there is not a back in the pattern, the judge will ask for it in one of the following ways:

1. Before or after the pattern work, the judge might ask the whole group of pattern riders who are lined up side by side to back as a group or one at a time as the judge walks down the line.

2. During rail work, the judge might request that the horses stop on the rail and back as a group on the rail.

3. After rail work, when the horses have come into the center of the ring to line up, the judge might ask the entire group to back together or one at a time as the judge walks down the lineup.

Whenever you are asked to back as part of a group, be sure to be aware of where other horses are. You might need to glance behind you on both sides before you begin. If you back into another horse, it could cause one or both horses to kick. Don't assume that the rider who is next to you in the lineup will back straight; he or she might back right into you and your horse. If you sense a problem will occur or is occurring, stop your horse and wait until the person next to you is finished backing. The judge will understand and appreciate your concern for safety.

B   **A**

C   **D**

E

F

A Jog

B Turn left

C Lope left lead circle

C Flying change

E Turn right

F Sliding stop

Back 5 steps

Walk

Join new lineup

PATTERN HELP

A Jog. Be ready at cone A when the previous rider is backing. Make your jog depart prompt and crisp. (See Pattern 9.)

B Turn left. Begin turning slightly before cone B so that your line makes a direct path to cone F. Keep the aids for 90-degree turn on the hindquarters left in mind as you make the turn. (See Patterns 3, 6, and 16.)

C Lope left lead. (See Patterns 4 and 19.)

Lope left circle. This is a small circle for a lope, so you will need to work in a collected frame. That makes it a bit more difficult to get a clean, forward flying lead change, so you will need to "open up" your horse on the last stride before the change. Do this by giving with your reining hand and inviting the horse to lope more forward. Be sure his body is straight before the change. (See Patterns 2 and 18.)

C Flying change to right lead. (See Pattern 33.)

E Turn right. (See Pattern 15.)

F Sliding stop. (See Tip at right.) After the stop, settle your horse for 1 to 2 seconds.

Back 5 steps. (See Pattern 7.)

Walk.

Join the new lineup.

TIP SLIDING STOP

A sliding stop begins with a gradual building of speed at the lope until the horse is galloping. Then the horse powers into a dramatic stop where the hind end drops low to the ground and the hind feet lock into position and slide forward. The horse's head and neck elevate to counteract the lowering of the hindquarters. The front feet continue to walk along as if the horse were swimming or pedaling.

The sliding stop is a trained maneuver, and you will need to ask your horse to stop the way he was trained. Generally, the sequence goes something like this:

- Keeping your seat light, drive the horse forward with both legs until the horse is running.
- Sit deep but don't throw your weight backward.
- Pick up on the reins.
- Some trainers also say "whoa" at the time they want the horse to plant its hind feet.
- When the horse stops and is sliding, either hold rein contact or begin to release it, according to the way the horse was trained.

A Walk 2 strides

Lope left lead

B Turn left

Flying change

C Stop

Back 4 steps

Walk forward 2 steps

360-degree turn on the
hindquarters to the right

Jog

Return to lineup

B

A

C

PATTERN HELP

A Walk 2 strides. (See Patterns 5, 6, 8, and 14.)

Lope left lead. (See Patterns 4 and 12.)

B Turn left. The sharper you are able to make this turn, the better shape you will be in to make your flying change where indicated. If you make a rounded corner, it will take you quite a few strides to get back on the straight line. (See Pattern 15.)

Just after the corner, flying change to right lead. Be sure your horse is straight and headed for the judge's belt buckle. Do not head to cone C. (See Pattern 33.)

C Stop. (See Pattern 5.)

Back 4 steps. After you back, you can pause 1 second before you step forward. This will allow you time to adjust your reins and seat. (See Patterns 6 and 14.)

Walk forward 2 steps. Don't pause after the walk. Use the forward motion to your advantage in the turn to come. (See Patterns 6 and 14.)

360-degree turn on the hindquarters to the right. Settle your horse for 1 second after the turn to be sure he is balanced and will strike off in a dignified jog. (See Pattern 32.)

Jog. (See Pattern 9.)

Return to the lineup.

TIP STOP–BACK–WALK–TURN–JOG

When you are faced with a portion of a pattern that has quite a number of things going on at one time like this sequence, rather than thinking of it as five or six different things to do, try to picture how it will all fit together.

First, what do all of these things have in common? The horse's body is absolutely straight. You will be applying very little rein or leg for bending.

Next look at what might seem natural and what might seem sticky. The lope to stop is a pretty well-practiced transition by now and a back from a stop is a very natural progression. It's a nice touch to ask for (allow) the rider to step forward after the back before beginning the 360-degree turn. This lets you establish a forward element to your turn that is sometimes hard to get right out of a back. If you establish this forward movement before starting your turn, the turn should flow, and while it is not supposed to be a turnaround (spin), it can be prompt in its execution. When you have finished the 360-degree turn and the horse is absolutely straight, pause for a fraction of a second and then jog off like you have somewhere to go.

So what you have is a straight line sequence of forward–stop–back–forward–turn–forward. It flows. Visualize this as a sequence, and it *will* flow.

Suitable for AHSA Stock Seat Open, Adult Amateur, and 11 and Over. A very fast pattern for large classes.

C

B

A

D

A Lope left lead

B Flying change

C Stop

  360-degree turn on the
    hindquarters to the right

  Lope left lead

D Sliding stop

  Back 8 steps

Pattern Help

A Lope left lead. (See Pattern 22.)

B Flying change to right lead. Here is one of those patterns that has a very specific spot where the flying change must occur — right next to cone B. That means you have to position your horse 1 stride before cone B and ask for the change at cone B. (See Pattern 33.)

C Stop. (See Pattern 5.)

360-degree turn on the hindquarters to the right. (See Pattern 32.)

Lope left lead. This can be a natural setup if you think about it beforehand. What you need to do is:

★ Keep your horse's body straight during the turn.

★ Finish a complete 360-degree turn on the line. (Your horse's weight will already be shifted over to the right at the end of the turn — perfect for the pre-lope position.)

★ Apply aids for lope left lead.

D Sliding stop. (See Pattern 40.)

Back 8 steps. (See Tip at right and Pattern 50.)

TIP | **YOUR HORSE'S TAIL: MISSING IN ACTION**

This pattern is a killer on long beautiful tails. If you show a Western Riding, Reining, or Horsemanship horse, you will be required to stop and back. Sliding stops and long backs are the biggest threats to a long tail and can make a horse reluctant to back. When the horse stops, his hindquarters drop, so the end of his tail is often laying on the dirt. When the horse starts backing, it is easy for him to step on the end of his tail and pull out large hunks all the way up to the dock. It doesn't take too many occurrences to result in a very thin tail. And when a horse steps on a large hunk of hair and yanks it out, it hurts. It could make him shy of backing in the future. Horses also can pull out large sections of tail when they are unloading from a trailer. That's why the tails of trailered horses are usually braided, wrapped, or bagged for loading, unloading, and traveling.

To protect your horse's tail, keep it trimmed so that the end is at the point of your horse's fetlock when the horse's tail is relaxed and flat on his anus (not raised). That way when your horse is working, it will be slightly above this point, which is a fairly safe level. A blunt cut tail (banged) is less wispy on the ends than a tapered tail so it tends to look thicker, and it's easier to keep trimmed regularly.

A Back

B 180-degree turn on the hindquarters to the left

Lope left lead

C Flying change

Counter-canter circle

D Stop

360-degree turn on the hindquarters to the right

Jog

E Stop

Pattern Help

A Back. When you start your line, remember to give yourself enough room so that when you turn at cone B you won't crunch the cone. (See Patterns 30 and 35.)

B 180-degree turn on the hindquarters to the left. (See Pattern 27.)

Lope left lead. (See Patterns 4 and 22.)

C Flying change to right lead. (See Pattern 33.)

Counter-canter circle to the left on the right lead. (See Tip at right.)

D Stop. (See Pattern 5.)

360-degree turn on the hindquarters to the right. (See Pattern 32.)

Jog. (See Pattern 9.)

E Stop. (See Pattern 3.)

TIP COUNTER-CANTER ON A CIRCLE

The counter-canter is not a lope on the wrong lead around a circle. It is a controlled and balanced exercise that shows great muscle development and a high level of training.

When you lope right lead, your horse should have a slight right bend (unless on a straight line such as here). When you lope right lead, your right seat bone should be ahead of your left seat bone. Weight should be deep in your right heel. Your right leg will be at the cinch to keep your horse slightly bent right. Your left leg will be behind the cinch to maintain the right lead.

When you counter-canter a circle to the left on the right lead, you want to maintain the above aids; the horse should be bent in the same direction as the lead — to the right. You want the horse to be looking slightly to the outside of the circle, but his body should be 100 percent on the track of the circle, not angled so his hindquarters drift in. Your rein aids will depend on the level of your horse's training but will generally be a light neck rein applied to the left side of the horse's neck. The goals of your rein aids are:

- To balance and direct the horse as he turns around the circle
- To keep him on the circle line
- To prevent the horse from overbending to the right

When counter-cantering:

- Keep your hips parallel to your horse's hips.
- Keep your shoulders parallel to your horse's shoulders.
- Be sure your horse doesn't speed up.

PATTERN 44

A Walk 2 strides

Jog

B Turn left

C Lope left lead circle

C Flying change

E Turn right

F Stop

Back 4 steps

Ride forward 2 steps

360-degree turn on the
hindquarters to the right

Jog to new lineup

Pattern Help

A Walk 2 strides. Be ready at cone A when the previous exhibitor is completing the 360-degree turn. (See Tip at right and Patterns 5, 6, 8, and 14.)

Then jog. (See Pattern 6.)

B Turn left. Focus straight for cone F. This will help you keep your lope depart straight. (See Patterns 3, 6, and 16.)

C Lope left lead. (See Patterns 4 and 19.)

Lope circle. (See Patterns 2 and 18.)

C Flying change to right lead. Prepare your horse for the change during the last stride of the left circle and ask for the change after the horse's entire body is straight on the line. (See Pattern 33.)

E Turn right. (See Pattern 15.)

F Stop. (See Pattern 5.)

Back 4 steps. (See Pattern 7.)

Ride forward 2 steps.

360-degree turn on the hindquarters to the right. (See Pattern 32.)

Jog to the new lineup. (See Pattern 9.)

TIP BE READY TO GO!

Since horse shows must keep moving, every effort you make to help things run more efficiently is appreciated. When you are next in line to perform a pattern and the judge looks over your way, you should be ready to go. Some judges might give you a little nod to indicate it's time to go, but because that can be tiring by the end of the day many judges just look your way and expect you to start the pattern.

When it is a multiple judge show, you should try to be sure all judges are watching you before you begin. If one judge is writing comments on the previous rider and you start before he or she is watching, part of your ride will be missed by that judge.

Generally, being ready to go means standing with your horse's ears at the starting cone.

Suitable for a state 4–H show pattern in which there are a large number of exhibitors

C

B

A

A Lope right lead

B Flying change

C Stop

Back 4 steps

360-degree turn on the
hindquarters to the right

Walk 4 strides

Jog

Join new lineup

PATTERN HELP

A Lope right lead. (See Pattern 22.)

B Flying change to left lead. (See Tip at right.)

C Stop. (See Pattern 5.)

Back 4 steps. (See Pattern 7.)

360-degree turn on the hindquarters to the right. (See Pattern 32.)

Walk 4 strides. (See Patterns 5, 6, 8, and 14.)

Jog. (See Patterns 4 and 6.)

Join the new lineup.

TIP | FLYING CHANGE TO LEFT LEAD

A flying change consists of a three-point check, pre-positioning aids, and the lead change itself.

Three-Point Check. As you are preparing for a flying change from right to left, you need to check three things:

1. Be sure your horse is loping a true 3-beat lope. If he is "4-beating," he won't have enough impulsion and his legs won't be in the right place at the right time for a change.
2. Be sure your horse's body is straight. It is much more difficult to get a clean, prompt lead change if your horse's spine is curved.
3. Be sure you feel contact with your horse through the reins. You should be able to further collect your horse by just moving your hand back 1 inch (2.5 cm). And if you move your hand forward 1 inch (2.5 cm), he should stretch forward.

Pre-positioning. Now, with your horse loping on the right lead, move your reining hand over to the right, which applies a left neck rein on the horse. You are shifting the horse's weight to his right side much like you do for a lope depart. At the same time, put your left leg on the horse to shift his weight right. When you are loping on the right lead, your right seat bone is more forward than your left seat bone. You can hold this pre-change position for 2 to 3 strides of lope at home if you want. At the show, you want to hone it down to 1 stride.

The Change. For the change, keep the horse straight and up on his right shoulder so his left shoulder is "free" to change. Do this by maintaining contact and using a slight left neck rein.

- Relax the pressure of your left leg that is holding the horse to the right (this "invites" the horse to the left), and move your left seat bone forward.

- Apply your right leg behind the cinch to ask for the change just as you would for a lope depart.

After the horse makes the change, you can initiate the new bend.

A Jog

B Stop

   360-degree turn on the
     hindquarters to the right

   Lope left lead

C Turn left

D Simple change through
    2 steps of walk

E Stop

   Back 4 steps

   Walk

   Return to lineup

C

B

A

D

E

Pattern Help

A Jog. For a change, the cone is on your left. Plan your line so that you don't "cone crunch" at cone B. (See Pattern 9.)

B Stop. The cone is on your left, and you must give your horse enough room so that when you perform the turn he doesn't step on the cone. If you miscalculate and are too close when you get to cone B, it would be better to sidepass a step or two before the 360-degree turn than it would to step on the cone. (See Pattern 3.)

360-degree turn on the hindquarters to the right. (See Pattern 32.)

Lope left lead. (See Pattern 42.)

C Turn left. The cone is on your left. (See Pattern 15.)

D Simple change through 2 steps of walk to right lead. The cone is on your right. (See Pattern 16.)

E Stop. The cone is on your right. You should stop when your horse's ears reach the cone. (See Pattern 5.)

Back 4 steps. (See Pattern 7.)

Walk.

Return to lineup.

TIP — AVOID STIFFNESS

Both on the rail and in the individual works, if you try too hard to assume correct posture you could become stiff. Tension inhibits fluid communication from your aids to the horse and results in several problems. First, it can actually work against your attempt at a correct position. Tension on the stirrup treads or gripping with the knees can lift you right out of the saddle and result in a loose seat. A rigid back doesn't flow with the stride of the horse and communicates tension to the horse. Tight neck and shoulder muscles do not allow your arms to hang relaxed or your upper body to respond to the changes in direction and speed of the horse.

An effective rider must be relaxed and follow the movements of her horse. A rigid wrist, caused from trying to hold the hand steady, prevents smooth communication with the horse's mouth via the bridle. Often this creates anxiety in the horse, which will manifest in such things as anticipation of lead changes, nervous tail swishing, avoidance of the action of the bit by "getting behind it," and an overall choppy performance.

Relax. Don't sweat the small stuff. It's all small stuff. The big stuff comes much later.

F
D
E
B
A

C

A Jog

C Lope left lead

D Stop

   Back 4 steps

E 360-degree turn on the
   hindquarters to the left

   Lope right lead

F Pattern finished

PATTERN HELP

A Jog. (See Pattern 9.)

B Continue jogging and make a half circle. Note that C is an imaginary spot directly across from cone B. That means you can theoretically make the circle any size you want. Choose a size that best showcases your horse's stride and your skills. (See Patterns 2 and 18.)

C Lope left lead. Control the second half of the circle to match the first half. (See Patterns 4 and 19.)

D Stop. (See Pattern 5.)

Back 4 steps. (See Pattern 7.)

E 360-degree turn on the hindquarters to the left. (See Pattern 27.)

Lope right lead. This is a natural setup. What you need to do is:

★ Keep your horse's body straight during the turn.

★ Finish a complete 360-degree turn on the line. (Your horse's weight will already be shifted over to the left at the end of the turn — perfect for the pre-lope position.)

★ Apply aids for lope right lead.

F Pattern finished; lope through the marker. After cone F, lope a few more strides around the corner, then break to a walk as you approach the new lineup.

TIP | **YOUR HORSE: YOU GOTTA LOVE HIM**

We would all like to have the perfect horse and the very best of tack to help us exhibit our skills. However, when you make the most out of the horse and tack you have, it shows. If you have pride in the thoroughness of your training and work with your horse, it will be evident in your riding skills. No amount of spray sheen or silver can outperform a practiced rider.

However, if you have advanced past your horse's capabilities and can comfortably afford to work your way up to the next level of horse and tack, you will have earned it and will continue to do well. On the other hand, if you look at a high-priced horse and expensive tack as a way to succeed without hard work, though you might win some of the time you will be losing out on the much greater reward — the satisfaction of achieving the goal yourself.

B

A

A Jog 4 steps

Extend the jog

B Stop

360- plus 90-degree turn on
the hindquarters to the left

Lope left lead

C Stop

Back 4 steps

Walk

Find a place on rail

C

PATTERN HELP

A Jog 4 steps. This is 2 strides, which takes about 16 feet (4.9 m). (See Pattern 9.)

Extend the jog. Save room to resume a regular jog for 1 to 2 strides before the stop. (See Pattern 24.)

B Stop. (See Pattern 3.)

360- plus 90-degree turn (1¼ turn) on the hindquarters to the left. You can approach this as a continuous turn of 1¼ rotations or as one full 360-degree turn followed by a quarter (90-degree) turn. (See Pattern 90.) As long as you perform smoothly and your riding shows finesse and planning, either method should work well. If your horse has had some reining training, the continuous turn is the way to go. Just be careful not to ask for too much promptness or you might end up with a spin! If, on the other hand, your horse walks slowly and carefully in his hindquarter turns, you would be better off performing a perfect 360-degree turn, then pausing a fraction of a second while you regroup and then perform the 90-degree turn as a link to the lope left lead. (See Pattern 31.)

Lope left lead. (See Pattern 27.)

C Stop. (See Pattern 5.)

Back 4 steps. (See Pattern 7.)

Walk.

Find a place on the rail.

TIP TAIL SWISHING

While you are standing on the rail waiting for the patterns to be completed, is your horse driving you nuts with tail swishing? One of the biggest and most obvious causes of tail swishing is flies. Be sure you've used an effective fly repellent on your horse's belly, the backs of his fetlocks and pasterns, his cannons, his entire neck and chest, and his chin and face.

If you are riding a mare and she is in season, she could be swishing her tail because she is antsy, excited, irritable, or looking for a stallion. If you have a mare that comes unglued when she is in heat, you can either leave her home on show day, talk to your veterinarian about medical or surgical alternatives, or put up with her PMS — Pouting Mare Syndrome.

Tail swishing is also an irritated reaction to cues, usually spurs. The horse's body language is saying, "Okay, I'll do it, but basically I don't like you cueing me there!" Be sure you have thoroughly accustomed your horse's sides to leg aids and the use of spurs so that he isn't hypersensitive to leg cues.

Walk to cone A

A Lope left lead

B Stop

   270-degree turn on the
     hindquarters to the left

   Counter-canter circle

B Flying change

A Stop

   Back 5 steps

   Find a place on rail

PATTERN HELP

Walk to cone A. (See Patterns 5 and 8.)

A Lope left lead. (See Pattern 12.)

B Stop. (See Pattern 5.)

270-degree turn on the hindquarters to the left. (See Pattern 31.)

Counter-canter a circle to the left on the right lead. The circle is designed to be as big as you need to keep your horse in counter-canter. Of course, the smaller the circle you ride, the more you are exhibiting your skill and the thoroughness of your horse's training and development. (See Pattern 47.)

B Flying change to left lead. (See Pattern 45.)

A Stop. (See Pattern 5.)

Back 5 steps. (See Pattern 7.)

Find a place on the rail. Jog or lope to quickly make way for the next exhibitor.

TIP SIMULTANEOUS FLYING CHANGE

A simultaneous flying lead change is one where a horse changes leads in his front legs and his hind legs at the same time. This is the smoothest and most technically correct flying change as the change does in fact, take place in the air ("flying") rather than on the ground.

When a horse changes leads in the front legs first and then on the next stride or two picks up the change in the hind, this is very undesirable. It means that the horse is heavy on his forehand and has dropped his shoulder in the change.

When a horse changes leads in the hind first and then on the next stride picks up the change in the front, it is not as bad as a front-first change because it is at least in the order the legs work — from back to front. But it still is not as fluid and smooth as a simultaneous change.

C   **B**   **A**

D

A Walk

B Jog

C Lope left lead

D Counter-canter circle

E Stop

    180-degree turn on the
      hindquarters to the right

    Lope right lead

F Stop

    Back 6 steps

    Walk

    Return to lineup

F

E

PATTERN HELP

A Walk. With the cone on your right, walk to cone B. (See Pattern 8.)

B Jog. Pick up a jog promptly at cone B because you will need to lope in just a few strides at cone C. (See Pattern 6.)

C Lope left lead. After you lope, you will need to turn taking care to make your next line so that cone D is on your left. (See Patterns 4 and 19.)

D Counter-canter circle. The size of this circle to the right on the left lead is not denoted by a cone. Choose a size that your horse can perform well without executing a flying lead change, breaking to a jog, or counter-cantering in poor, stiff form.

Lope to cone E.

E Stop. (See Pattern 5.)

180-degree turn on the hindquarters to the right. (See Pattern 28.)

Lope right lead. (See Pattern 28.)

Turn right. You'll have to gauge your turn so that you head dead center for cone F. This is one pattern where you head straight for the cone to stop, not alongside it. (See Pattern 15.)

F Stop. (See Pattern 5.)

Back 6 steps. (See Pattern 7.)

Walk. (See Patterns 5 and 8.)

Return to the lineup.

TIP PREVENTING LOCKUP ON AN EXTENDED BACK

The key to preventing lockup during backing is to have a good starting point. At the beginning of a back, adhere to the following criteria:

- The horse is straight.
- You are sitting with equal weight on both seat bones.
- Your legs are both at the cinch, passive at the moment.
- You have contact with the horse's mouth.
- The horse is rounding into the contact; that is, he is flexing vertically at the jaw, poll, and throatlatch; the topline of his neck is slightly arched; and his back is flat or raised.

English Equitation

English Equitation usually refers to Hunter Seat Equitation but can also refer to Saddle Seat Equitation or Dressage Equitation. Much of the information presented in this book's Introduction is also applicable to English Equitation. Specifics are noted here.

HUNTER SEAT EQUITATION

Hunter Seat Equitation is the English style of riding that is suitable for fox hunting, showing a hunter, or jumping.

General Position and Seat. The rider should have an effective, polished appearance, with seat and hands light and supple, conveying the impression of complete control should any emergency arise. The eyes should be up and the shoulders back. When viewed from the front or rear, the rider's seat legs and upper body should be symmetrical from left to right with weight evenly distributed on each side.

Legs. The toes should be at an angle best suited to the rider's own conformation, ankles flexed in slightly toward the horse's side, heels down, and the side of the calf (not the back of the calf) of the leg in contact with the horse and slightly behind the girth. The ball of the foot should be on the stirrup iron. The iron must not be tied to the girth. Toes can be parallel to the horse's sides or slightly turned out, but if extremely turned out the back of the calf will be on the horse's side, which is heavily penalized. Viewed from the side the rider's

knee and toe are in one vertical line, and another vertical line should bisect the rider's shoulder and hip and touch the back of the rider's heel.

Legs too far forward are worse than legs too far back. Legs in proper position but that have no contact at the calf are worse than legs in proper position that have no contact at the knee. The latter condition is seen with long-legged riders on narrow-bodied horses.

Arms and Hands. Hands should be over and in front of the horse's withers, with knuckles 30 degrees inside the vertical and hands slightly apart and making a straight line from the horse's mouth to the rider's elbow. The method of holding the reins is optional, and the bight (ends) of the reins may fall on either side. However, all reins must be picked up at the same time; this is called addressing the reins. The contact with the horse's mouth should be definite without being rigid. There should be a sensitive communication with the horse using subtle rein aids.

Mounting and Dismounting. To mount, take up reins in the left hand and place that hand on the withers. Grasp the stirrup leather with the right hand and insert the left foot in the stirrup and mount. To dismount, you may either step down or slide down. The judge will take the size of the rider into consideration when evaluating mounting and dismounting.

Position in Motion. At the walk, the upper body should be vertical. At the posting trot, it should be inclined forward 20 degrees in front of the vertical. At the sitting trot, it should be vertical or 5 degrees in front of the vertical. At the extended trot, you should post. At the canter, the upper body should be 5 to 10 degrees in front of the vertical. At the hand gallop, gallop and jumping, you would assume the two-point position, which is 30 degrees in front of the vertical. In the two-point position, the top part of the pelvis tilts forward, lifting your weight off the horse's back and transferring it to your legs. Hands should be forward, up the horse's neck but not resting on the horse's neck.

SADDLE SEAT EQUITATION

Exhibitors of American Saddlebred, Arabian, and Morgan horses often show their horses under saddle seat tack and corresponding attire. Many of the comments in Hunt Seat Equitation are applicable to Saddle Seat Equitation.

In Saddle Seat Equitation classes, riders should convey the impression of effective and easy control. The rider should show the judge that he or she has the ability to present a horse. The judge will, in effect, be answering the question, "Which rider would I want to have showing my own horse?"

To show a horse well, the rider should show evidence of ring savvy. Is the horse being shown to his best advantage? Is the rider in complete control of the situation? Judges look for a performance that is an overall picture of competence.

The seat of the Saddle Seat Equitation rider should in no way be exaggerated, but it should be thoroughly efficient and comfortable for riding the animated horse at any gait and for any length of time.

To obtain proper position, place yourself comfortably in the saddle and find your center of gravity by sitting with a slight bend at the knees, without use of irons. While in this position, adjust the stirrup leathers to fit. Irons should be placed under the ball of the foot (not under the toe or with the foot "home"). You should have even pressure on the entire width of the sole of your boot and the center of the iron. Foot position must be natural (neither extremely in nor extremely out). There should be a straight line from your shoulder through your hip to your heel. Your posture should be straight but not rigid. There should be a slight bend at your knee with the grip being in the thigh and knee, never with the calf. The calf should be in position to give signals, not held out from the horse's barrel in an exaggerated manner. The foot and ankle position should not be distorted.

Hands should be held in an easy position, neither perpendicular nor horizontal to the saddle, and should show sympathy with the horse's mouth, adaptability, and control. The height that the hands are held above the horse's withers depends on how and where the horse carries his head. The method of holding the reins is optional, except that both hands must be used and all reins must be picked up at one time. The bight of the reins should be on the off side.

Position in Motion. At the walk, the upper body is vertical and there should be a slight motion in the saddle. At the trot, there should be a slight elevation from the saddle when posting; hips should stay under the body, with neither a mechanical up-and-down motion nor a swinging forward and backward. At the canter, you should have a close seat, going with horse.

The rail work called for is the same as for Hunter Seat Equitation, but the style is more elevated, animated, and flashy without becoming exaggerated or extreme. The performance should be formal yet light, crisp yet correct, exuberant yet easy. The rider should give the overall impression of competency with style and polish.

DRESSAGE EQUITATION

All of the movements of the dressage equitation rider should be obtained without apparent effort. The rider should be well balanced with supple lower back and pelvis, steady thighs and legs, and legs that are stretched downward. The upper body remains vertical in all gaits and should be free, easy, and erect. In Dressage Equitation, all trot work is executed sitting unless otherwise indicated. The hands should be low and close together without touching each other or the horse. The thumb should be the highest point. The elbows and arms should be close to the body, enabling the rider to follow the movements of the horse smoothly and freely and to apply his aids imperceptibly. Only the rider who is able to relax and contract his lower back muscles at the right moment is able to influence the horse correctly.

Undesirable Horsemanship and Equitation and areas that receive penalties and disqualification are discussed in the Introduction. Rider problems specific to English Equitation include:

★ No contact on the reins; loose as in Western Pleasure

★ Rider loses stirrup(s), then grips with knees

★ Posting on the wrong diagonal

★ Exaggerated posting (incline, height, and/or landing)

★ Broken line at the wrist ("puppy paws")

★ Hands bobbing

★ Too much weight in stirrups

★ Lower legs flap as rider rises to post

★ Excessive curve in lower back

CLASS ROUTINE

AHSA rules apply to Hunter Seat Equitation and Saddle Seat Equitation for Arabian, Saddlebred, Morgan, and all breeds in Dressage Equitation. In stock horse breed Hunter Seat Equitation classes, the association rules apply and are very similar in routine to Western Horsemanship classes.

In AHSA English Equitation classes, all of the contestants enter the ring at a walk or trot. The group rail work comes first and consists of working both ways of the ring at a walk, trot, and canter. The reverse may be made toward or away from the rail. The horses are backed in the lineup.

If time permits, the judge then asks the riders being considered for an award to perform at least two of the tests listed in the rule book. Only tests listed in the book may be used. The tests may be performed individually or in a group at the judge's discretion. Instructions must be publicly announced. If a pattern is used, it must be posted at least 1 hour prior to the beginning of the class. A pattern is defined as two or more tests.

Performance Around Ring. This involves the rider working on and off the rail, performing such maneuvers as trot, halt, rein back, canter a circle, trot, and return to the lineup. This type of test is difficult and time-consuming and is usually reserved for a championship or medal class.

GAITS

Gaits are the natural footfall patterns of the horse, such as walk, trot, canter, and gallop.

Walk. The walk is a natural, flat-footed 4-beat gait where the horse moves straight; that is, his hind feet follow the lines of travel of his front feet. Flat-footed means the hoof lands flat, not toe or heel first, which would indicate that the horse is verging on a trot, jigging, or prancing. The horse's expression at the walk should be alert, with a reasonable length of stride in keeping with the size of the horse. In most cases the hind feet should step into or in front of the prints left by the front feet.

Trot. The trot is a smooth, energetic, forward-reaching 2-beat diagonal gait. The trot should be very even in rhythm from one diagonal pair of legs to the other. The horse should track straight with the hind feet following in the tracks of the front feet. When a trot is called for in English Equitation, unless otherwise noted, it is to be a posting trot, with the rider posting on the correct diagonal.

Posting accomplishes two important tasks. When a horse is working on a curve or circle, his inside hind leg is carrying more weight so it requires more effort to push off. Also, the outside shoulder and foreleg need to make a larger circle than the inside shoulder and foreleg when turning. Posting reduces the work of the inside hind leg by removing the rider's weight during push off. Posting also frees the outside shoulder and foreleg to allow maximum reach.

Posting is traditionally taught by getting in rhythm with the outside foreleg with the easily remembered phrase "Rise and fall with the leg on the wall."

When the horse is circling clockwise, the rider should be on the left diagonal — sitting in the saddle when the left front leg is on the ground. When the horse is circling counterclockwise, the rider should be on the right diagonal: the rider should be sitting in the saddle when the right front leg is on the ground.

Extended Trot. The extended trot is an increase in stride length without an increase in rhythm. The legs don't move quicker but the legs do reach farther, resulting in a longer, more ground-covering stride.

Canter. The canter is a smooth, ground-covering 3-beat gait that is rhythmical but not fast. When a horse is moving to the left, he should be on the left lead unless a counter-canter has been requested. When moving to the right, he should be on the right lead. If a horse is cantering with 4 beats, he is not performing a true gait and will be penalized. In Equitation classes, a rider should be able to easily feel this and correct it by pushing the horse on.

Counter-Canter. The counter-canter is a deliberate, balanced canter on one lead while the horse is traveling in a curve in the opposite direction. For example, in a circle to the left, when you ask the horse to canter on the right lead, you are asking him to counter-canter. When counter-cantering, there should be no change in rhythm or stride, and the horse should be flexed and bent slightly toward the lead. When a horse can canter on the lead opposite to the direction of travel, he is exhibiting great training, balance, and strength. It is a maneuver that shows if a horse is just performing robotically or if the rider is effectively guiding the horse.

Extended Canter. The extended canter is an increase in stride length without an increase in rhythm. The legs don't move quicker, but they do reach farther, resulting in a longer, more ground-covering stride.

Hand Gallop. The hand gallop is called for in Hunter Seat Equitation and is ridden in two-point position. It is essentially an extended canter.

Rein Back Saddle Seat. The rein back is a 2-beat diagonal gait in reverse. A rein back will almost always be asked for in the individual pattern work or else it will have to be asked for in the group rail work. First, the horse must be stepped up from his stretched position. Then the required steps backward are taken, and the horse is halted and then sent forward to retrace the same number of steps. The horse is then halted and parked. The judge will be looking for the proper adjustment from the rider if the horse attempts to step sideways.

Rein Back Hunter Seat and Dressage. The horse's feet are raised and set down in distinct diagonal pairs. Starting from a square halt, the horse should retain contact with the bit and flex poll and neck softly in response to the rider's hand aids. The horse's legs should move straight back without any sideways deviation. Faults in the rein back include anticipation, resistance (head up, back hollow), evasion of the rein aids (behind the bit or tilting the head), stepping sideways, or dragging the forefeet.

MOVEMENTS

Movements test a rider's control and precision in the application of all aids. Movements include changes in direction, speed, and length of stride during movement, and turns and backing following a halt.

Straight Lines. The horse should track straight. His head and neck should be straight in line with his body while performing straight lines.

Curved Lines. The horse's head and neck should be slightly bent to the inside on curved lines and circles, and his entire body should be similarly curved.

Serpentine. A serpentine is a snakelike pattern that can be a shallow wave or a series of half circles connected by straight lines.

Circle. A circle should be evenly round and the two halves of the circle should be equal in size. Circles should be performed at the appropriate speed, size, and location as dictated by the pattern.

Figure 8. A figure 8 consists of two circles that touch at a flat spot in the center (about one stride long) resulting in a figure that looks like the number eight.

Halt. A halt should be straight, square, prompt, and smooth, and the horse's body should remain straight during the entire movement. The horse's back should round, not hollow, during a halt. His head position should remain relatively consistent.

Turn. Turns should be smooth and continuous and contain the appropriate bend for the curvature of the figure.

Turn on the Forehand. When performing the turn on the forehand, the horse rotates around a pivot point, which is the front leg of the direction of the turn. In a turn on the forehand left, the pivot point is the left front leg, the horse is bent to the left, and his haunches move to the right. As the haunches move to the right, the left hind crosses over and in front of the right hind. In a turn on the forehand right, the haunches move left.

Turn on the Haunches. When performing the turn on the haunches, the horse should walk around the inside hind leg and cross the outside front leg over the inside front leg.

Sidepass. In a sidepass, the horse's body is straight or very slightly counterflexed, and he steps directly sideways. In a sidepass to the right, the left legs cross over in front of the right legs as the horse moves sideways.

Two-Track. In a two-track, the horse moves forward and laterally on a diagonal line with the horse's body bent away from the direction in which he is moving.

Leg Yield. In a leg yield, the horse moves forward and laterally in a diagonal direction with the horse flexed opposite to the direction he is moving.

Simple Change. A simple lead change is a change from one lead at the canter to the other lead at the canter, with a prescribed number of walk or trot strides in between (usually 1 to 3) or a halt in between the leads. The change should be executed precisely, with the exact number of designated strides or steps, and at the designated location. The change should occur smoothly.

Flying Change. A flying lead change is a change in the air, during the moment of suspension between 2 canter strides, from one lead at the canter to the other lead at the canter with the change occurring simultaneously with the front and rear legs. The change should be executed smoothly, without an increase in speed, with the horse's body straight, and at the designated location.

Any Other Test. In some rule books, the phrase is "any other test or maneuver" included to allow the judge to add any riding test to the pattern that he or she deems appropriate.

Change of Diagonal. To change from one diagonal to another when changing bend or when dictated by pattern instructions, the rider sits 2 beats (most common) or rises for 2 beats (less common) and then resumes posting.

Addressing the Reins. With your horse standing at a square halt, place the buckle just ahead of the horse's withers. Pick up the buckle with your right hand and lift the reins about 2 inches (5.1 cm). Place your left hand over the reins in this manner: Put your little finger on one side of the left rein and your ring finger on the other side. Put your index finger over on top of the right rein, which places your middle finger underneath the right rein. Your thumb will be underneath all to complete the grip.

With the reins positioned in the fingers of your left hand, draw the reins up with your right hand as you slide your left hand forward. As you pull smoothly, keep your right hand low; don't raise it high in the air. When you have almost made contact with the horse's mouth, you will drop the bight of the reins on the horse's neck. If you are riding Saddle Seat, the bight goes on the off side. If you are riding Hunter Seat or Dressage, either side is acceptable although the off side is traditional.

Then take the right rein from your left hand and assume proper hand position. Addressing the reins is an organized, proficient way to attain gradual, even contact with the horse's mouth.

If a whip is carried, it should be held in the left hand as the reins are being threaded with the right hand. This test is usually used for riders under age 13.

Feet Disengaged from Stirrups/Feet Engaged. In some rule books, this test can only be conducted in the lineup with the horses standing. The purpose is to see if a rider can easily find a stirrup by feel, without looking or requiring assistance from the hand. In some instances this test can be called for on the rail at the walk, trot, or canter. If riders are asked to drop their irons during rail work, they usually leave them down so that they can be picked up later in the test.

Ride without Stirrups. In most rule books, it is permissible for the judge to require the riders to perform any pattern without stirrups. If riders are asked to perform without irons, they can either leave the stirrup leathers down or cross them over the horse's withers. The left iron hangs on the right side of the horse's withers; the right iron hangs on the left side of the horse's withers. In some instances, riding without stirrups is prohibited for young riders. Riding without stirrups at the trot is to test if the rider is posting correctly from the thigh and knee. The idea is to assess the rider's balance and correctness; it is not an endurance and fitness test.

Demonstrating Simple Change of Lead. Changes down the center line are slightly easier to perform than changes down the rail because the horse tends to associate the rail with a particular lead. When the rail is on the horse's right, habit tells him he should be on the left lead. All leads should be taken with the horse's body parallel to the rail, not angled toward or away from the rail. If a judge requires three lead changes beginning with the left lead, you will have to perform four canter departs to demonstrate the three changes — from left to right, right to left, left to right.

Demonstration Ride of Approximately 1 Minute on Your Own Mount. This test may be used in advanced classes to give the rider the opportunity to show what he or she and the horse can do best. The rider provides a written copy of the demonstration to both the judge and the announcer. The ride is timed and judging stops after 1 minute, but the rider is not penalized if the demonstration runs over 1 minute as long as the test is completed as written. It is better for a rider to do a simple test well than a complicated one poorly.

USUALLY NOT ALLOWED

If you are showing at a sanctioned show, certain tests are usually not allowed because of safety and time considerations. However, if you are at an open show, you might be asked to perform one of the following tests.

Asking Riders to Mount or Dismount. Due to time constraints and the difficulty some younger riders have mounting larger horses, mounting and dismounting as a test may be prohibited in your rule book.

Asking Riders to Exchange Horses. A test of true horsemanship is to see a rider perform well on another exhibitor's horse. This was a popular test in the past, but due to increased concerns with safety and time, it is usually prohibited. The purpose of this test is to see which riders have the capability to adapt to a different horse. This is rarely used and then only to separate the top two riders in a major competition. The riders are usually not asked to perform a test with an unfamiliar horse that they have not already performed with their own horse.

STEPS AND STRIDE FOR GAITS AND MANEUVERS

GAIT OR MANEUVER	NUMBER OF STEPS	LENGTH OF STRIDE (AVERAGE)
Walk	4	6' (1.8 m)
Trot	2	10' (3.1 m)
Extended trot	2	12' (3.7 m)
Canter	3	12' (3.7 m)
Extended canter	3	14' (4.3 m)
Gallop	4	14' (4.3 m)
Rein back	2	5' (1.5 m)
Turn on the forehand, turn on the haunches	4	N/A

NUMBER OF STRIDES IN VARIOUS SIZED CIRCLES

DIAMETER	CIRCUMFERENCE	NUMBER OF STRIDES (AVERAGE)
20' (6.1 m)	63' (19.2 m)	11 at walk 6 at trot 5 at canter
30' (9.2 m)	94' (28.7 m)	16 at walk 9 at trot 8 at canter
50' (15.3 m)	157' (47.9 m)	26 at walk 16 at trot 13 at canter
66' (20.1 m)	207' (63.1 m)	35 at walk 21 at trot 17 at canter

Beginning English Equitation Patterns

Beginning patterns are suitable for any rider just starting out. They require the basic gaits: walk, trot, and canter and the rein back. There are no simple or flying lead changes, no extended gaits, and no turns on the forehand or haunches. The rider must know how to post properly on the correct diagonal and change diagonals.

The level of a pattern does not necessarily relate to the age of rider. At a show, beginning patterns are not necessarily synonymous with younger riders. In some shows, the age 14 and under riders are so accomplished that they would require advanced patterns to separate them in terms of skills. On the other hand, some groups of novice amateur riders over age 35 might be overly challenged with an intermediate pattern but would do nicely with a beginning pattern.

On the following page, you'll find four blank arenas where you can record patterns that you've ridden at shows.

TRAINING NOTES

COMPETITION GOALS

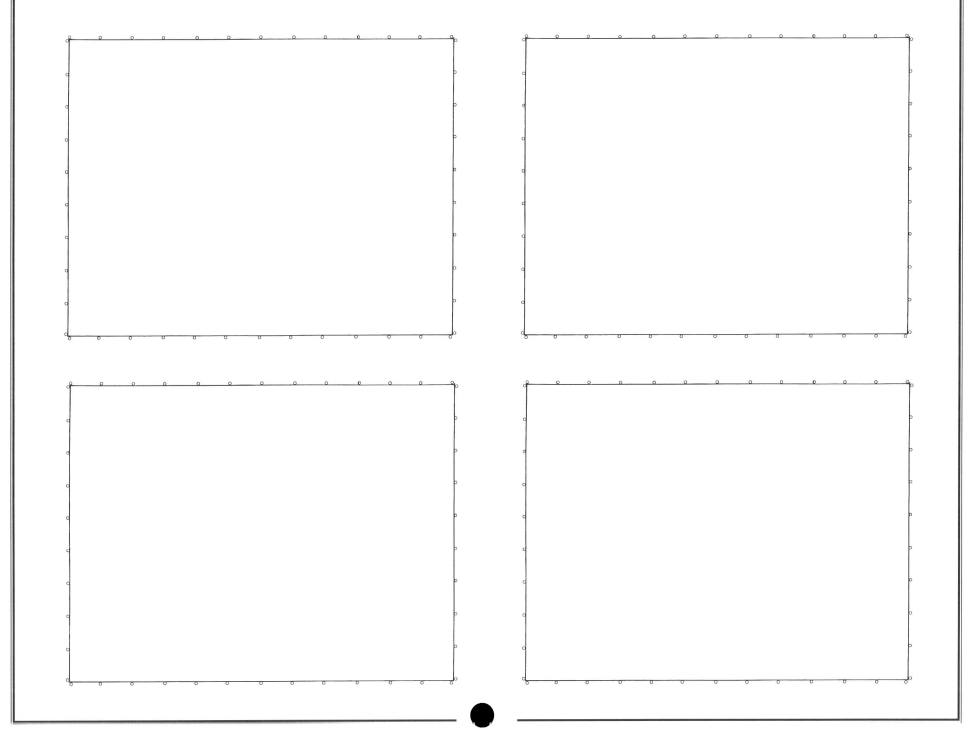

PATTERN 51

X Trot left circle

X Trot right circle

X Halt

Stand for 3 seconds

Return to lineup

Pattern Help

Since this pattern is designed for beginning riders, safety is emphasized. The judge might require one exhibitor to be completely finished with the pattern and be back in the lineup before the next rider begins to go on course. This pattern begins and ends at the center of the figure 8. The portion where the rider approaches and exits the figure 8 is not judged. But it still pays to ride it as if it were.

If the show pace is moving along quickly, however, you will want to be ready when it is your turn. Start your horse moving out of the lineup when the previous rider has finished the halt and is returning to the lineup. I suggest you walk out of the lineup, post the trot to X, and continue trotting. There are no cones to help or hinder you. You will use the position of the judge as a reference point for the center of your figure 8.

X Trot circle to the left. X is an imaginary point. The trot is a 2-beat diagonal gait that has a good degree of forward impulsion. Whenever trot is indicated, it is to be a posting trot unless otherwise stipulated.

Be sure to know your left from your right because even if you ride beautifully, if you go to the right first it will cost you points. As you finish your left circle, try to ride your horse straight for one moment before you start the right circle. (See Pattern 59.)

X Trot circle to the right. Try to match the size of the circle that you rode to the left. (See Tip at right.)

X Halt. Stand for 3 seconds. A halt is the English term for a stop. (See Patterns 54 and 70.)

When 3 seconds are up, you can **leave the pattern by walking, trotting, or cantering back to the lineup.** However, when you get close to the line, be sure to drop down to the walk so that you don't disrupt any other horses in the line.

Note: This pattern does not contain a canter or back, so there will be rail work. (See Pattern 69.)

TIP CIRCLE SIZE AND SHAPE

In a pattern like this, there are no cones to indicate the size of the circles. Therefore, unless the judge tells you otherwise before the class begins, you could ride any size circles you want. Bigger circles require less sharp turning and are easier for beginning riders or stiffer horses, but they take longer to ride. Smaller circles are quicker to ride because you are covering less ground, but the horse must be collected and flexible in order to bend more sharply.

You don't need to know how large in feet (or meters) the circle will be. What you need to know is what size circle you can make *smoothly*. And you must be able to make the same size circle in both directions. Some horses are stiffer in one direction and want to make a huge circle, but in the other direction they want to curl up and make a tiny circle. You need to make both circles the same size and a nice, uniformly round shape. A circle should be uniformly round, not egg-shaped or oblong or flat on one side. You will need to use sideways glances with your eyes and peripheral vision to help you plan and ride a round circle.

B

A

C

A Trot

B Turn left

C Halt

Stand for 3 seconds

Walk

Find a place in new lineup

PATTERN HELP

Line your horse up so that he is facing down the pattern line with his front feet about 5 feet (1.5 m) from cone A; the tips of his ears about 3 feet (.9 m) from the cone. When the judge looks at you and it is time for you to go, squeeze your horse's ribs with both legs to ask him to walk. As soon as he starts at the walk, squeeze him again, harder, for the trot. This should result in him walking about 3 to 4 steps before he starts trotting. He should be trotting when you pass cone A.

A Trot. Keep cone A on your right side. Although you want your horse to be trotting with energy, you don't want him to trot fast or it will be hard for you to post properly and to make a smooth turn. Aim straight toward cone B, but turn before you get to it. Just before cone B, gather your thoughts and your horse, but not so much that you cause him to walk. (See Pattern 59.)

B Turn left. Turning should be a smooth, continuous arc. The horse should not speed up, slow down, or get stiff. Let your eyes (not your head) go to cone C just before you turn left. (See Patterns 54 and 56.)

Use a left direct rein and right supporting rein; weight your left seat bone; bring your right shoulder forward. When you are halfway through the turn, begin straightening or you will overturn. Aim straight forward knowing that you want to halt with cone C on your right.

C Halt. Stand for 3 seconds. Once your horse has halted, you should release your active aids. You should relax your legs, seat, and release a little contact on the reins. You want the horse to be in "neutral," so your aids should be "neutral," too. (See Patterns 54 and 70.)

Walk. When 3 seconds are up, squeeze with both legs to cause your horse to walk. As soon as he takes the first few steps, begin turning him to the right. After you've walked a few steps, the pattern is over and the judge will be watching the next exhibitor. (See Pattern 60.)

Find a place in the new lineup.

Note: This pattern has no canter or back, so there will be rail work. (See Pattern 69.)

TIP POSTING

When a horse trots, he uses his legs in diagonal pairs. The left front and right hind lift and land together, and the right front and left hind lift and land together. When a horse travels to the left (counterclockwise), making a series of left turns, his left hind reaches farther forward and does more work supporting and driving that the right hind. And the right front must make a larger arc than the left front on a circle or turn. To lessen the workload of the inside hind leg and to allow the outside foreleg move freely forward, English riders post.

When you post, you alternately rise and sit in time with the outside foreleg. As the outside foreleg reaches forward, you should rise; as the outside foreleg lands, you should sit. Remember to "rise and fall with the leg on the wall." This requires a good sense of feel. At first you might want to quickly glance downward without lowering your head to check the front leg movement.

Post on the right diagonal when going to the left (counterclockwise), which means you rise and fall with the right front leg. When going to the right (clockwise), rise and fall with the left front leg, which is posting on the left diagonal.

A Trot right diagonal

B Change diagonals

C Change diagonals

D Halt

PATTERN HELP

This pattern has no cones, just imaginary points. This requires you to have a strong picture in your mind of the size of the arena, where the judge is standing, the starting point, the ending point, and what you need to fit in between.

A Trot right diagonal. Since you will be making a turn to the left from A to B, you will want to post on the right diagonal. Sit as the right front lands and rise as the right front reaches forward. You will be using left direct rein and right supporting rein. You'll weight your left seat bone and apply your left leg at the girth. (See Patterns 52 and 59.)

B Change diagonals. Sit 2 beats when you pass B, and change bend from left to right. Now you will use right direct rein and left supporting rein. You'll weight your right seat bone and apply your right leg at the girth. Be sure you are making the loops of this exercise deep enough so that they look like curves, not straight lines. (See Tip at right.)

C Change diagonals. Sit 2 beats when you pass C and change bend from right to left.

D Halt. To halt, as you approach D, sit deep in the saddle, look straight ahead, increase pressure on the reins by squeezing your fist or pulling straight back slightly, about 1 to 2 inches (2.5–5.1 cm) at the most. Sit with equal weight on both seat bones and look straight ahead between your horse's ears. Take care not to let your hands drift off to the left or the right or this might make your horse halt crooked. (See Pattern 54.)

Note: This pattern does not contain a canter or rein back, so expect rail work in at least one direction. (See Pattern 69.)

TIP CHANGE OF DIAGONAL

In English Equitation patterns, when a diagonal is not specified you should post according to the turn. However, in some instances, the judge wants you to post on a straight line and may designate a particular diagonal. When you change direction or change diagonals, you sit 2 beats and then begin posting again. This will put you on the new correct diagonal. If you sit 3 beats, you will be on the old diagonal again. One of the most important skills of the English Equitation rider is to know his or her diagonals. It is ideal that when you begin posting you start on the correct diagonal. However, if you start out on the wrong diagonal for 1 stride, then sit 2 beats to correct it, a judge will not discredit you strongly because at least you demonstrated an awareness of the incorrect diagonal and knew how to correct the situation.

PATTERN 54

A Trot

B Turn left

X Trot left circle

X Change diagonals

Trot right circle

X Halt

Walk

Return to lineup

Pattern Help

A Trot. (See Pattern 59.)

B Turn left. (See Tip at right and Pattern 56.)

X Trot left circle. (See Pattern 51.)

X Change diagonals. (See Pattern 53.)

Trot right circle. (See Pattern 51.)

X Halt. You don't want to surprise your trotting horse with a sudden pull on the reins for a halt. Instead, prepare him for the halt:

- ★ Keep your upper body straight.

- ★ Still your seat; don't post or follow the movement of the trot anymore.

- ★ Keep both of your legs on the horse's sides at the girth.

- ★ Move your hands straight backward 1 to 2 inches (2.5–5.1 cm).

- ★ As soon as the horse has "started to halt," begin easing the aids.

Walk. (See Pattern 60.)

Return to the lineup.

Note: This pattern does not contain a canter or rein back, so expect rail work in at least one direction. (See Pattern 69.)

TIP TURNING

To make a controlled left turn at cone B, imagine you were turning in the corner of an arena:

- Move your right shoulder forward, which will cause more weight to be on your left seat bone.

- Deepen your left knee and keep your heel down to prevent your left side from collapsing.

- Look slightly to the left as you turn.

- Use your left leg at the girth to help bend the horse.

- Use your right leg slightly behind the girth to keep the horse's haunches on the line.

- Use a left direct rein and a right supporting rein.

C   **B**   **A**

D   **E**

A   Walk

B   Trot

C   Canter left lead

D   Walk

E   Halt

     Rein back 4 steps

PATTERN HELP

Note that the first three cones of this pattern are located outside the arena.

A Walk. (See Pattern 60.)

B Trot. (See Pattern 56.)

C Canter left lead. To ask your horse to canter, use two sets of aids: first, a set of positioning aids, then the aids for the canter. For the positioning aids, you want to get the horse ready for the lead you want. For the left lead, you want to shift your horse's weight over to the right side of his body momentarily. If you move his weight over to the right side of his body for a fraction of a second, you are lightening his left side, which will make it easier for him to take the left lead. You do this mainly by applying your left leg at the girth. You might also need to apply a little more right supporting rein than usual to help hold his forehand over to the right. As soon as you feel he has done this, which should just be 1 second, it's time to use the aids for the canter.

The aids for the canter left lead are:

★ Right leg behind the girth with a rolling forward feeling from your right seat bone (which is farther back) to your left seat bone (which is farther forward)

★ Left seat bone forward with weight in your left stirrup and a lowered knee and heel

Once your horse is cantering, add the left bend and make a nice rounded shape, making sure that you are planning to make your next transition alongside cone D. (See Tip at right.)

D Walk. (See Pattern 67.)

E Halt. (See Pattern 67.)

Rein back 4 steps. (See Patterns 58 and 74.)

TIP TROT TO CANTER

To give you an idea of how long it takes to apply the aids for the canter, say, "Position aids, canter," and in the time it takes you to say those words, you should have applied the position aids and then cantered. If you take too long with the positioning aids your horse will "stall out."

This is a fairly sophisticated transition for a beginning rider, but it's best if you learn it correctly. And if you are ready to show, you should know the correct way. That way, in the more advanced patterns you will be able to canter on any lead at any time.

TIP DETERMINING LEFT LEAD

The left lead canter is a 3-beat gait with the following footfall pattern:

1. Right hind
2. Left hind and right front
3. Left front

When your horse is traveling to the left, he should be on the left lead. His left front leg will reach farther forward than this right front leg. Without moving your head, glance down at your horse's shoulders to see which shoulder is moving farther ahead. That is what lead your horse is on. Register what that feels like in your seat and legs so that later you can tell just by feeling what lead your horse is on.

D

B

C

A

A   Walk 2 strides

B   Trot around cone B

C   Canter left lead

D   Halt

Rein back 4 steps

Pattern Help

A Walk 2 strides. (See Pattern 60.) A stride is one complete set of steps. In the walk, 1 stride is a complete 4-beat revolution of the horse's legs: left hind, left front, right hind, right front. To count 2 strides, count every time you feel a particular hind leg reach forward: left hind 1, left hind 2. If you have not developed feel yet, you can glance down at a front leg to measure: left front 1, left front 2. Eventually, you should train yourself to count strides by feel through your seat so that you can most effectively communicate with your horse.

Trot, then turn left. (See Tip at right and Pattern 54.)

B Trot around cone B. As you trot your horse in a gentle bend around the cone be sure that:

★ His poll stays at a consistent level. If it drops way down, it means he is heavy on his forehand or getting behind the bit. If he raises up way up, it indicates resistance to your reining aids.

★ He maintains a steady rhythm. If he speeds up, it means he is losing his balance. If he slows down, he is confusing your reining aid for turning with one for slowing down or halting.

★ As you bend him to the left, his head and neck turn slightly to the left. When you change the bend, his head and neck turn slightly to the right.

C Canter left lead. Be sure to straighten your horse's body and shift the weight over to the right side of his body before you ask for the canter; otherwise, you might get a right lead instead of a left lead. (See Pattern 55.)

D Halt. (See Pattern 59.)

Rein back 4 steps. (See Patterns 58 and 74.)

TIP WALK TO TROT

You might think this is almost too simple to worry about, but it is one of the best elementary exercises to start collecting your horse and keeping him straight. When you ask your horse to trot by sitting deep in the saddle, squeezing with both legs at or slightly behind the girth, and giving a little forward with your reining hand, he should energetically reach under with his hind legs and lift his back. You should feel yourself rise a little as he takes off. This is a helpful hint — begin posting! If your horse's back stays flat or caves in when he starts to trot, it will be very difficult for you to post properly. You will need to practice many walk-trot-walk transitions at home. Every horse needs to learn how to round up underneath you and trot energetically, lift his back, and keep his body straight.

C
⊙

B
⊙

A
⊙

D
⊙

E
⊙

A Walk

B Trot left diagonal

C Canter left lead

D Trot right diagonal

E Halt

Rein back 4 steps

PATTERN HELP

Since horse shows must keep moving, every effort you make to help things run more efficiently is appreciated. When you are next in line to perform a pattern and the judge looks over your way, you should be ready to go. Some judges might give you a little nod to indicate it's time to go, but because that can be tiring by the end of the day many judges just look your way and expect you to start the pattern.

When it is a multiple judge show, you should try to be sure all judges are watching you before you begin. If one judge is writing comments on the previous rider and you start before he or she is watching, part of your ride will be missed by that judge.

Generally, being ready to go means standing with your horse's ears at the starting cone.

A **Walk.** (See Pattern 60.)

B **Trot left diagonal.** (See Patterns 52 and 56.)

C **Canter left lead.** (See Pattern 55.)

D **Trot right diagonal.** (See Tip at right.)

E **Halt.** (See Pattern 54.)

Rein back 4 steps. (See Patterns 58 and 74.)

TIP CANTER TO TROT

In a downward transition from a canter to a trot on a straight line, your seat bones, shoulders, and legs should be fairly even and symmetrical. If anything, in this left lead pattern your left shoulder and seat bone might be slightly ahead, but if they are more than an inch or two, that is undesirable. Also, your right leg will be slightly behind the girth. To prepare for the downward transition to a balanced, symmetrical trot, you will want to "square up;" that is, move your right leg up to the girth so that it's directly across from your left leg, square up your shoulders, and be sure you feel weight evenly on your seat bones. Quit following the 3-beat canter rhythm with your seat, and imagine you are cantering uphill. Maintain a still seat, flex your abdominals, and move your hands about 1 inch (2.5 cm) toward your waist. As soon as the horse trots, yield with your hands slightly and follow the 2-beat trot motion with your seat for 1 to 2 beats before you begin posting.

E

D

C

B

A

A Walk 2 strides

Trot

Canter right lead between
cones C and D

E Halt

Rein back 4 steps

PATTERN HELP

A Walk 2 strides. That's 8 beats or about 12 feet (3.7 m). If you find that it's difficult or impossible to fit 2 strides into this pattern as drawn, either walk 1 stride and begin your serpentine on time or walk 2 strides and begin your serpentine late. (See Pattern 14 for some other options.) It would be hard for me to predict which way the judge at your show might rule, but I suggest walking 1 full stride, then squeezing your horse into a trot while you begin your serpentine. Be sure to keep your poise about any discrepancies like this. (See Patterns 56 and 60.)

Trot. (See Pattern 56.)

Trot around cone B. Change diagonals as you pass cone B. (See Patterns 54 and 56.)

Trot around cone C. Change diagonals as you pass cone C. (See Patterns 54 and 56.)

Between cones C and D, canter right lead. You should ask for the canter on the small "straightaway" between the loops around cones C and D. At that one moment, the horse is straight, not bending right or left. He has just finished bending left and after the canter will bend right. Should you ask for the canter slightly ahead of or after the straightaway? Your pre-canter positioning aid shifts the weight of the horse momentarily away from the lead you will be asking for. So in this case, since you'll be asking for a right lead, you will position the horse's weight off to the left before you give the canter aids. That means it would be logical to position your horse for the canter just before the straightaway while he is just finishing up a left bend as this will help you shift his weight to the left. Then you can ask for the right lead in the straightaway and things will click. If instead, you position the horse in the straightaway and then ask for the canter when you start turning right, you might have an awkward reaction from your horse and get the wrong lead. (See Pattern 55.)

E Halt. (See Pattern 59.)

Rein back 4 steps. (See Tip below.)

TIP REIN BACK 4 STEPS

When your horse performs a rein back, he should pick up two legs at a time (right front and left hind) and reach backward with them and set them down. As he is setting them down, the other diagonal pair (left front and right hind) will lift, reach back, and set down. If a horse drags his feet backward through the dirt, it shows the horse is very lazy and has not been taught to step backward with energy. If a horse takes very tiny steps backward, it means he is being resistant to the rider's aids.

It is easy to count 4 steps while reining back. Every time your horse picks up one diagonal pair of legs and moves it back, you will feel it in your hips. Your pelvis will rock back and forth from side to side as he steps back. You can count something like this: "Left rear 1, right rear 2, left rear 3, right rear 4." And that would be the 4 steps back. If you need to look at the shoulder to learn how to feel, you can count like this: "Left front 1, right front 2, left front 3, right front 4." And that would be the 4 steps.

A Trot

B Canter left lead

C Halt

Rein back 4 steps

Walk

Return to lineup

PATTERN HELP

A Trot. To start your pattern off with a sparkle, you should really perfect the halt to trot transition. Think "Spring ahead!" as you apply the following aids:

★ Maintain contact with the reins as you would in a halt.

★ Hug the horse's sides and abdominals with your lower legs to cause him to lift his back and get light.

★ Then apply intermittent "squeeze, squeeze, squeeze" (not kick, kick, kick) with your legs as you lighten your seat and your horse will spring into a trot. As soon as you feel the trot begin to happen, post, then check your diagonal and change if necessary to get on the correct diagonal.

The reason you need to maintain contact with the reins (unlike giving with the reins as you do for a halt-to-walk transition) is that you want the horse to strike off energized, somewhat collected, and round into your hands with the first step. You don't want him to lower his head and neck, so you must "keep him on the aids" for takeoff.

B Canter left lead. (See Pattern 55.)

C Halt. (See Tip below.)

Rein back 4 steps. (See Pattern 58.)

Walk. (See Pattern 60.)

Return to the lineup. Although this portion of the pattern is not being judged, you still want to maneuver properly. If you are the first in the lineup, halt your horse perpendicular to the arena end in a way that the line won't cause problems for those who are performing the pattern. If you are next in line, "park" your horse parallel to the first horse but with adequate space between you for safety. If you and the other rider reached out your arms toward each other and they touched, you would be too close.

TIP CANTER TO HALT

In beginning patterns, a judge would rather see you perform a canter to trot to halt in good form than an abrupt canter to halt in poor form. However, the rider who can perform a canter to halt in good form will earn the most points because this is what is asked for. If you yank abruptly on the reins, you will startle your horse and he will most likely throw his head up, open his mouth to avoid the harsh action of the bit and stiffen into a very unglamorous halt of sorts. To avoid this, properly prepare your horse:

• Keep your upper body straight, with your shoulders over your hips.

• During the portion of the canter stride when your seat is going down, still the motion of your seat; don't continue following the motion of the canter.

• Keep both your legs on the horse's sides at the girth to keep him straight.

• Move your reining hand straight backward 1 to 2 inches (2.5–5.1 cm).

• As soon as the horse has halted, ease up on your aids.

C

B

A

Walk to cone A

A Trot

B Canter left lead

C Halt

Rein back 4 steps

Walk

Exit arena at any gait

PATTERN HELP

Walk to cone A. Be ready in the lineup so that as the rider before you is finishing, your horse is attentive and ready to walk. This takes practice and timing. If you get your horse "too ready," he might walk or turn in anticipation and you will have a poor start. (See Tip at right.)

A Trot. Begin the trot as soon as your horse's head passes cone A. Remember, cone A is to your left. As you trot toward cone B, remember to keep it to your right. Just as your horse's head passes cone B, you should canter. That means you must prepare your horse 1 stride before with the positioning aids. (See Pattern 56.)

B Canter left lead. The canter depart should be prompt and the horse's body should be straight. (See Pattern 55.)

Canter balloon. Since this shape is an odd-shaped circle, I call it a balloon. You will canter your horse for 1 or 2 strides straight before you begin the circle portion. As you finish the circle portion, you want to plan ahead so that when you straighten you will be heading on a straight line that will pass right next to cone C, with cone C on your right. As you are cantering the final straightaway, be sure your horse's body is absolutely straight by having even contact on your six points: two reins, two seat bones, and two legs. Gather him slightly, but not too much or he might trot. (See Pattern 60.)

C Halt. (See Pattern 59.)

Rein back 4 steps. (See Pattern 58.)

Walk. (See Pattern 60.)

Exit the arena at any gait. This means you can exit the arena at the gait of your choice: a walk, trot, or canter. Choose a gait that you feel is safe for you. You don't want to choose the canter if you think your horse will get excited when he sees the open gate and bolt out of the arena. On the other hand, walking out of a big arena will take quite a bit of time, which might delay the next rider from starting.

TIP WALK

The walk at the beginning and end of this pattern is an important indicator of your ability as a rider. It can be difficult to take a quiet, relaxed horse out of a lineup where he is comfortably standing next to other horses and have him walk off straight and with energy. Practice this at home. Halt your horse and have him stand for several minutes, then walk him off. Do this many times so that you'll see how much leg and seat are necessary. Sometimes you might be standing in an equitation lineup for 15 minutes or more before it is your turn.

At the end of the pattern, after the rein back, you will want to walk your horse a few strides to show that after the canter, halt, and rein back, your have control of your horse and can calmly walk away. You will need to do this on light contact. If you have to hold the horse strongly with the rein, it shows a lack of practice and control.

PATTERN 61

C   B   A

D   E

A Trot left diagonal

B Change diagonals

C Canter left lead

D Trot right diagonal

E Halt

Rein back 4 steps

Halt and address the reins

Pattern Help

Note that the first three cones are set outside the arena.

A Trot left diagonal. (See Pattern 56.)

B Change diagonals. Sit 2 beats and change to the right diagonal. (See Pattern 53.)

C Canter left lead. (See Pattern 55.)

D Trot right diagonal. (See Pattern 57.)

E Halt. (See Pattern 54.)

Rein back 4 steps. (See Pattern 58.)

Halt and address the reins.

TIP ADDRESSING THE REINS

With your horse standing at a square halt (see Pattern 71 for a description of a square halt), place the buckle just ahead of the horse's withers. The buckle joins two English snaffle reins together. The horse is now standing "on the buckle" with loose reins.

Pick up the buckle with your right hand and lift the reins about 2 inches (5.1 cm). Place your left hand over the reins in this manner: Put your little finger on one side of the left rein and your ring finger on the other side. Put your index finger over on top of the right rein, which places your middle finger underneath the right rein. Your thumb will be underneath all to complete the grip.

With the reins positioned in the fingers of your left hand, draw the reins up with your right hand as you slide your left hand forward. As you pull smoothly, keep your right hand low; don't raise it high in the air. When you have almost made contact with the horse's mouth, drop the bight of the reins on the horse's neck. If you are riding Saddle Seat, the bight goes on the off side. If you are riding Hunter Seat or Dressage, either side is acceptable although the off side is traditional.

Then take the right rein from your left hand and assume proper hand position. Addressing the reins is an organized, proficient way to attain gradual, even contact with the horse's mouth.

You will need to practice at home to make sure your horse will stand perfectly still "on the buckle" while you address the reins. Many horses will walk off or turn when they are put on the "honor system" of no contact, so you must make a formal lesson of this at home to ensure it won't be an error or safety issue at a show.

You'll find addressing the reins easiest if you choose a rein length that is appropriate for your horse's neck length and your arm length. It will be very difficult to address the reins properly if the reins are too long. Keeping the reins clean and supple will make them glide and flow easily during the exercise.

Most often, the request to "address the reins" is made verbally by the judge at the end of your pattern or in the group lineup. It is not usually written as part of the pattern.

A Trot left diagonal

B Canter right lead circle

B Trot right diagonal

C Halt

Rein back 4 steps

Walk

Find a place on rail

PATTERN HELP

A Trot left diagonal. (See Pattern 59.)

B Canter right lead. Use and say "Positioning aids, canter." For right lead positioning aids, move the horse's weight over to the left side of his body. Immediately apply the aids for the canter.

The aids for the canter right lead are:

★ Right seat bone forward with weight in your right stirrup and a lowered knee and heel

★ Left leg behind the girth with a rolling forward feeling from your left seat bone (which is farther back) to your right seat bone (which is farther forward). (See Pattern 55.)

Canter a circle to the right. Be sure to start and finish the circle at cone B. The size of the circle is up to you as there are no markers to indicate size. Choose the size circle that your horse can canter without speeding up, breaking to a trot, or stiffening. Usually a 50-foot (15.3 m) diameter circle works well. (See Pattern 51.)

B Trot right diagonal. Trotting at the same time you are finishing a circle and starting and keeping a straight line takes some coordination. (See Pattern 57.)

C Halt. (See Pattern 59.)

Rein back 4 steps. (See Pattern 58.)

Walk. (See Pattern 60.)

Find a place on the rail.

TIP RIGHT LEAD

The right lead canter is a 3-beat gait with the following footfall pattern:

1. Left hind
2. Right hind and left front
3. Right front

When your horse is traveling to the right, he should be on the right lead. His right front leg will reach farther forward than his left front leg. Without moving your head, glance down at your horse's shoulders to see which shoulder is moving farther ahead. That is what lead your horse is on. Register what that feels like in your seat and legs so that later you can tell just by feeling what lead your horse is on.

B

A

A Trot left diagonal

Change diagonals

Walk

B Turn left

Canter left lead

C Halt

Rein back 4 steps

C

Pattern Help

Note the first two cones of this pattern are set outside the arena.

A Trot left diagonal. (See Pattern 59.)

Change to right diagonal. (See Pattern 53.)

Before cone B, walk. To perfect the trot-to-walk transition, you're going to have to practice this a lot at home. In this pattern, because you will have to turn as soon as you make your transition, you must be certain you can do these things in short order. The key to getting a forward walk from a trot is that as soon as you feel your horse "begin to stop trotting," you need to release your restraining aids. Here's what I mean:

★ Quit following the trot with your seat; still your seat.

★ Draw your hands back toward your waist about 1 to 2 inches (2.5–5.1 cm).

★ Immediately when you feel your horse gets the signal to "power down a notch" you must:

  Move your hands forward toward your horse's mane about 1 to 2 inches (2.5–5.1 cm) to allow your horse to lower and reach with his neck for the walk.

  Initiate and follow the 4-beat walk tempo with your seat.

  Keep your legs evenly on your horse to keep him straight.

B Turn left. (See Patterns 54 and 56.)

Then canter left lead. (See Tip below.)

C Halt. (See Pattern 59.)

Rein back 4 steps. (See Pattern 58.)

TIP WALK TO CANTER

You have already been practicing the trot-to-canter transition, so you know that you need to first apply positioning aids and then immediately the canter aids. The same goes here. The only difference is that now you must also apply a little more impulsion to get your horse to strike off into a clean canter. And you need to hone your precision so that everything runs like clockwork.

For a walk to canter left lead, first shift your horse's weight over to his right side. That's left leg at the girth and possibly a little stronger right supporting rein. Instantly when you feel the weight shift, apply the canter aids: your right seat bone and leg should be deep and slightly behind the girth, sending energy rolling forward diagonally forward to the left seat bone, which is slightly ahead of the right seat bone.

It's time to say something about your shoulder and canter departs. Generally, your shoulders will automatically be over your hips, so if your right seat bone is back your right shoulder will be slightly back and so on. For the left canter depart, your left shoulder would be slightly ahead of the right shoulder for the depart, but as soon as the canter is established the shoulders should once more be parallel. Try to keep your shoulders even most of the time. Never use exaggerated upper body twists to try to accomplish canter departs or other maneuvers.

A Walk 3 strides

Canter left lead

B Trot

Change diagonals

C Halt

Rein back 4 steps

Walk

Return to lineup

Pattern Help

Note that cone A is outside the arena to keep the rail clear for rail work.

A Walk 3 strides. (See Patterns 56 and 60.)

  Canter left lead. (See Pattern 63.)

B Trot. The diagonal is not specified here, but because you will be turning to the left you should post on the right diagonal. (See Pattern 57.)

  Change diagonals. (See Pattern 53.)

C Halt. (See Pattern 54.)

  Rein back 4 steps. (See Pattern 58.)

  Walk. (See Pattern 60.)

  Return to the lineup.

TRANSITIONS

The changes in gait and speed within a gait are the transitions. The connecting moment between a gait and a halt or another maneuver (such as a turn on the forehand) is also a transition. Transitions should be made precisely and smoothly — not abruptly — at the markers. The rhythm of a gait should be maintained right up until the transition. The rhythm should not quicken or slow down in anticipation of the change in gait. Before, during, and after the transition, the horse should remain consistent in form and maintain contact on the aids.

Intermediate English Equitation Patterns

Intermediate level is where most riders are. Intermediate patterns include everything in beginning patterns plus more difficult changes of diagonal, simple lead changes, 90- or 180-degree turns on the forehand, extended gaits, and halt from a canter.

On the following page, you'll find four blank arenas where you can record patterns that you've ridden at shows.

TRAINING NOTES

COMPETITION GOALS

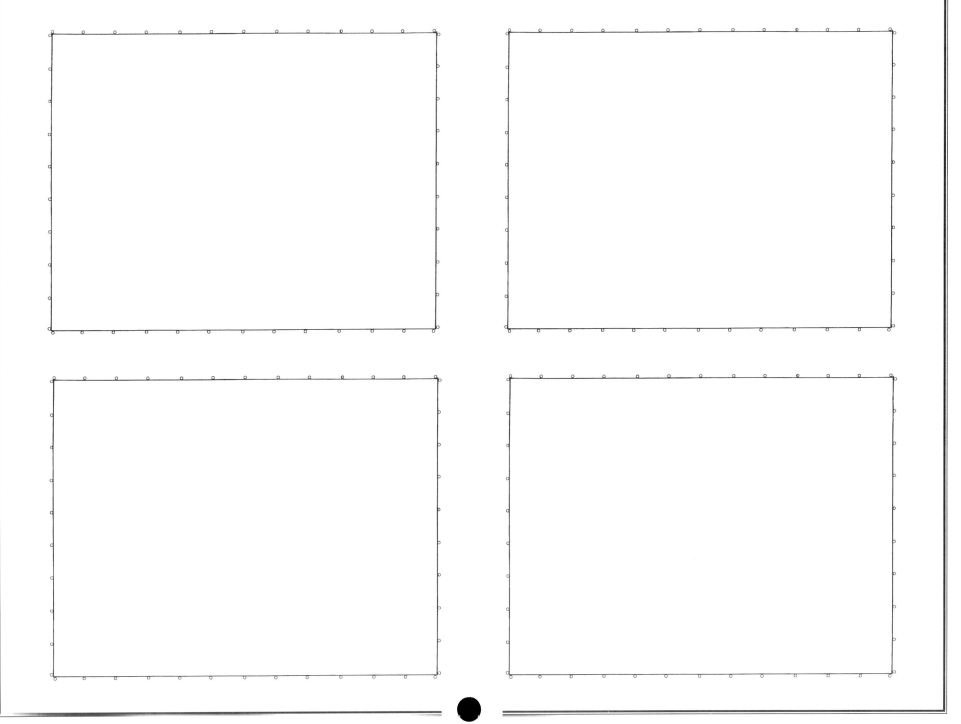

B

A

C

D

A Walk

B Trot

C Change diagonals

D Canter right lead

C Simple change

B Halt

   Rein back 5 steps

   Find a place on rail

Pattern Help

A Walk. Start your horse out like you are really walking somewhere. You have a lot of ground to cover, and if your horse is pokey at the walk it will be painfully obvious to you how long it will take to get to cone B. (See Pattern 60.)

B Trot. You are going to trot a half circle on the right diagonal before you change diagonals, so keep things fairly organized as you head toward cone C. (See Pattern 56.)

C Change diagonals. Sit 2 beats and resume posting, now on the left diagonal. (See Pattern 53.)

D Canter right lead. (See Pattern 55.)

C Simple change to left lead. (See Tip at right.)

B Halt. (See Pattern 59.)

Rein back 5 steps. (See Pattern 58.)

Find a place on the rail.

TIP SIMPLE CHANGE

A simple change is a change from one lead at the canter to the other lead at the canter usually with a halt or prescribed number of walk or trot strides in between. The change should be executed precisely, with the exact number of designated strides or steps and at the designated location. The change should occur smoothly. The horse's body should remain straight before, during, and after the change.

When a simple lead change is called for, it should be a simple lead change and not a flying lead change.

This pattern does not specify whether the change is to take place through a halt, walk, or trot, so the decision is up to each exhibitor. It also does not specify the number of steps or strides in between the leads so that also is up to the exhibitor, but no more than 3 strides should ever be used. Suggestions are:

- Canter–halt–position–canter
- Canter–walk 2 strides while positioning–canter
- Canter–trot 2 strides while positioning–canter

A

A   Canter right lead

     Simple change

B   Trot right diagonal

     Change diagonals

C   Halt

     Rein back 4 steps

     Walk

     Return to lineup

B

C

PATTERN HELP

A Canter right lead. This is almost an advanced maneuver because just as you begin turning the corner, you are counter-cantering for about 1 stride. (See Tip at right and Pattern 82.)

Halfway between cones A and B, simple change to left lead. It is not specified in the instructions whether the simple change is to be through a walk, trot, or halt. The drawing indicates a trot. If you have a question about any pattern, ask the judge. (See Pattern 65.)

B Trot right diagonal. (See Pattern 57.)

Halfway between cones B and C, change diagonals. (See Pattern 53.)

C Halt. (See Pattern 54.)

Rein back 4 steps. (See Pattern 58.)

Walk. (See Pattern 60.)

Return to the lineup.

TIP HALT TO CANTER

Everything you have learned about positioning aids and canter aids from the walk and trot apply here with modifications. When you ask a horse to canter from a standstill, you start with the horse standing with his four legs squarely underneath him.

When it is time to canter, you have to position him just like when he is moving at the walk or trot. When he is moving, it is not so noticeable that he shifts slightly over to his right before left lead aids are applied. But when he is at a standstill, it will be more noticeable that he shifts over to the right just before the depart. His body is straight yet you shift his weight over to the right just a fraction of a second before you apply the canter left lead aids. You'll be driving deeper with your right seat bone as you push his right hind leg deep under his body, reaching forward.

If you push just your horse's haunches over to the right so that he is standing on a diagonal line, he will canter crooked, like a crab. This is very undesirable. His body must be straight. You need to move his shoulder over as well as his haunches.

Don't be tempted to lean your upper body forward in an attempt to help "jump-start" him. This just squashes your horse out behind you. And don't rock or pump your upper body to try to get him started. At home you will need to work on providing the extra incentive through your aids that is necessary to get a canter from a halt while at the same time maintaining proper position.

A good exercise is canter-walk-canter-halt-canter with very little time in between transitions. You can practice this in one direction in the arena, asking for the same lead each time. Then reverse and practice it in the opposite direction on the other lead. Then practice on a straight line and alternate which leads you request to prevent your horse from anticipating.

PATTERN 67

A Trot left diagonal

B Change diagonals

C Canter left lead

D Simple change

E Walk

F Halt

   Rein back 3 steps

   Trot

G Walk

PATTERN HELP

This pattern has no cones. It is a free-form pattern that will test your ability to approximate the written pattern. When a judge uses a pattern like this, she is more likely interested in forward movement and good shapes. She'll expect absolutely silky-smooth transitions because she's letting you pick the moment they occur. Think of the pattern as straight lines down the long side and along the short end, followed by 2 half circles and straight work on the diagonal. Piece it together, and draw the picture in your mind.

A Trot left diagonal. (See Pattern 59.)

B Change diagonals. (See Pattern 53.)

C Canter left lead. (See Pattern 55.)

D Simple change to right lead. (See Pattern 68.)

E Walk. (See Tip at right.)

F Halt. (See Pattern 55.)

  Rein back 3 steps. (See Patterns 58 and 74.)

  Trot. The transition from rein back to trot is from a diagonal gait in reverse to a diagonal gait forward. If a horse is on the bit and collected, you will feel like you are springing forward when you trot. You should just let your horse's weight settle on the last rearward step and instantly be translated to the first forward trot step. Don't lean back when you are reining back, as it might cause the horse to hollow his back and place his hind legs way behind his back. He needs his hind legs well underneath himself to spring forward into a prompt trot depart. Also, you don't want to be "left behind the action." (See Pattern 98.)

G Walk, and exit the arena.

TIP CANTER TO WALK

In some ways, this is a more challenging transition than a canter to halt. You need to finish the circle at the canter with your horse still bent to the right. As you join the straight line, you will have to use slightly more left rein and right leg behind the girth to straighten your horse. At the same time you will need to move your left leg into a neutral central position. Still the motion in your seat for a brief instant as you draw your hands about 1 inch (2.5 cm) back toward your waist. When you feel the horse breaking down from the canter, get an even feel on both reins and begin the following motion of your seat to a 4-beat walk. If you get a stride of trot in between, keep your cool and get down to a walk as soon as possible, but with smooth application of the aids. I'd find it much less of an error if the transition were totally smooth and had 1 trot stride in between the canter and walk than if the horse halted abruptly and had to be urged on to walk. Of course, the ideal is a smooth transition directly from a canter to a forward, straight walk. This takes lots of at-home practice.

A   Trot right diagonal

B   Turn left

C   Canter left lead circle

     Simple change through
       3 strides of trot

E   Turn right

F   Halt

     Rein back 4 steps

     Walk

     Join new lineup

PATTERN HELP

A Trot right diagonal. (See Pattern 59.)

B Turn left. (See Patterns 54 and 56.)

C Canter left lead. There is no cone at C, so use cone D to gauge your takeoff and return point.

Canter circle. This pattern includes a cone to denote the size of the circle; the circle is to be made *inside* the cone. The circle is relatively small, about 30 feet (9.2 m) in diameter. This means it has a 94-foot (28.7-m) circumference. You should be able to fit about 8 strides at the canter in this small circle. This requires you to be accurate with your canter depart so that you don't lose any footage there by trotting past C. Also, your horse will have to be collected and quite supple in his bending and on the bit; this is not a circle to ramble on. (See Pattern 51.)

Simple change through 3 strides of trot. Since the trot is a 2-beat gait, 3 strides require 6 beats. The diagonal pair in canter left lead is the left hind and right front, and when the horse breaks down from the canter they will be the first diagonal pair to land for the trot. If you count that diagonal pair as beat 1, that means beat 6 is right hind and left front. Since the left hind is the initiator of the canter right lead, that means the horse has to canter right after beat 5 of the trot. What all this means is that you have to position your horse during beat 5 and give the canter aids during beat 6. Your horse will drive farther under than usual with his left hind. (See Pattern 62.)

E Turn right. (See Tip at right.)

F Halt. (See Pattern 59.)

Rein back 4 steps. (See Pattern 58.)

Walk. (See Pattern 60.)

Join the new lineup.

TIP | TURNING A CORNER AT A CANTER

You've cantered around the corner of an arena many times, but this turn at cone E is much sharper. You shouldn't be cantering fast, but you will want to stay relatively tight to the cone to demonstrate your skill and control. To do this, you must intensify your normal "cornering techniques." When you're loping right and you ride deep into an arena corner, your aids are:

- Look to cone E as you begin the turn.
- Sit deep on your right seat bone, with your right shoulder back and left shoulder forward.
- Lower your right heel and knee.
- Bend your horse to the right with a right direct rein and a left supporting rein to prevent him from overbending and popping his right shoulder out in a bulge.
- Use your right leg at the girth to give the horse a point to bend around.
- Have your left leg ready slightly behind the girth to prevent the haunches from swinging off the track to the left.

To make a sharp turn, use the same aids but at double intensity for the 2 or 3 strides going into and around the corner. Relax the aids as you are coming out of the corner.

PATTERN 69

A Trot left diagonal

Change diagonals

B Turn left

X Canter right lead circle

X Simple change through
2 steps of walk

Canter circle

X Walk

Return to lineup

B

A

D

C

PATTERN HELP

A Trot left diagonal. (See Pattern 59.)

Change diagonals. Since you will be making a turn to the left, change to the right diagonal. (See Pattern 53.)

B Turn left. (See Patterns 54 and 56.)

X Canter right lead. X is an imaginary point with no cone, so use cones C and D to gauge its location. If the judge is standing directly across from cone B, that will give you an additional reference point. (See Pattern 55.)

Canter circle between X and cone D. (See Pattern 51.)

X Simple change through 2 steps of walk. (See Tip at right.)

Canter circle between X and cone C. (See Pattern 51.)

X Walk. Your horse might be anticipating a halt here, so be sure you focus forward and walk. (See Pattern 67.)

Return to the lineup.

Note: This pattern does not contain a rein back, so the judge will ask for it in one of the following ways:

1. Before or after the pattern work, the judge might ask the whole group of pattern riders who are lined up side by side to back all at once as a group or one at a time as the judge walks down the line.

2. During rail work, the judge might request that the horses stop on the rail and back as a group on the rail.

3. After rail work, when the horses have come into the center of the ring to line up, the judge might ask the entire group to back together or one at a time as the judge walks down the lineup.

Whenever you are asked to back as part of a group, be sure to be aware of where other horses are. You might need to glance behind you on both sides before you begin. If you back into another horse, it could cause one or both horses to kick. Don't assume that the rider next to you in the lineup will back straight; he or she might back right into you and your horse. If you sense a problem will occur or is occurring, stop your horse and wait until the person next to you is finished backing. The judge will understand and appreciate your concern for safety.

TIP | **SIMPLE CHANGE THROUGH 2 STEPS OF WALK**

Just as you finish the first circle and have straightened your horse, you will need to drop to a walk for 2 steps and then strike off on a canter left lead. You are essentially going from right bend to straight at the same time you are performing a downward transition. Then immediately you perform an upward transition to canter at the same time you go from straight to left bend. You won't be able to easily count 2 steps of walk in between two canter circles, so you will have to go on instinct and feel. As soon as your horse drops down from a canter to a walk, you should give him the aids for the next canter. That means the pre-canter positioning aids must be applied during the last few strides of the "old" lead.

PATTERN 70

A Trot left diagonal

B Change diagonals

Turn left

C Canter left lead

D Simple change through 2 steps of walk

E Halt

Stand for 3 seconds

Rein back 5 steps

Walk

Return to lineup

Pattern Help

A **Trot left diagonal.** Normally when you head in this direction in an arena, you would post on the right diagonal, but this pattern asks for the left diagonal to begin with. (See Pattern 50.)

B **Change diagonals.** At cone B, sit 2 beats and resume posting on the right diagonal before you begin the turn at the corner. (See Pattern 53.)

Turn left. (See Patterns 54 and 56.)

C **Canter left lead.** (See Pattern 55.)

D **Simple change through 2 steps of walk to right lead.** (See Pattern 69.)

E **Halt.** (See Pattern 59.)

Stand for 3 seconds. (See Tip at right.)

Rein back 5 steps. (See Pattern 58.)

Walk. (See Pattern 60.)

Return to the lineup.

TIP STAND FOR 3 SECONDS

It is up to you to determine how long 3 seconds are; the judge is not responsible for telling you. Say to yourself, in your mind, without moving your lips, "One thousand one. One thousand two. One thousand three." And it will be close enough to 3 seconds.

TIP USING THE VOICE

Using the voice in any way or making clicking, clucking, or kissing sounds is a serious fault and will detract from the rider's overall performance and score. Although you might have used the voice command "whoa" to train your horse, it is best not to use it in the show ring. A horse should stop from your seat, leg, and rein aids.

A Trot left diagonal

B Change diagonals

C Turn left

Walk

D Canter right lead

E Halt square

Pause

Rein back 4 steps

Walk

Return to lineup

C **B** **A**

D

E

Pattern Help

A Trot left diagonal. Normally when you head in this direction, you would be posting on the right diagonal, but this pattern starts off on the left diagonal, so you must demonstrate both diagonals and a change. (See Pattern 59.)

B Change diagonals. Sit 2 beats and resume posting on the right diagonal. (See Pattern 53.)

C Turn left. (See Patterns 54 and 56.)

Walk. (See Pattern 63.)

D Canter right lead. (See Pattern 63.)

E Halt square. (See Tip at right.)

Pause. A pause should be 1 to 2 seconds, just long enough to show the judge that you have trained your horse not to anticipate reining back.

Rein back 4 steps. (See Pattern 58.)

Walk. (See Pattern 60.)

Return to the lineup.

TIP SQUARE HALT

A square halt is one where the horse's body is directly on the line of the pattern. His hind legs are directly behind his front legs, not offset to the left or right. His cannon bones are vertical. This puts his front legs next to each other and directly below his shoulders, not propped in front or angled behind. His hind legs are next to each other, and the cannons are positioned directly below his hocks or set just a bit under, but they are not camped out or angled excessively under. The square halt is a balanced, collected, planned halt, which shows great conditioning and training.

At home you might want a friend to tell you when your horse's legs are square so you can register the feeling. In the show ring, never look down to see if the horse's legs are square!

PATTERN 72

A Walk 3 strides

Trot left diagonal

B Change diagonals

C Canter left lead circle

Simple change through
3 steps of trot

D Canter right lead circle

E Halt

Rein back 4 steps

Walk

Return to lineup

Pattern Help

A Walk 3 strides. That is 12 beats, which require about 18 feet (5.5 m). (See Patterns 56 and 60.)

Then trot on left diagonal. Usually when headed in this direction, you'd be trotting on the right diagonal, but a change is planned. (See Pattern 56.)

B Change diagonals. Sit 2 beats and resume posting on the right diagonal. (See Pattern 53.)

C Canter left lead circle. When you are at the midpoint of the circle, look to the straight line to be sure you are going to join it where you left it. (See Pattern 55.)

Simple change through 3 steps of trot. Three steps of trot are 1½ strides, which require about 15 feet (4.6 m). You must position your horse for the right lead during steps 1 and 2, and give the aids for the canter right lead during step 3. (See Patterns 68 and 74.)

D Canter right lead circle. Gauge your circle size and shape so you rejoin the straight line at the correct point. (See Pattern 51.)

E Halt. (See Pattern 59.)

Rein back 4 steps. (See Pattern 58.)

Walk. (See Pattern 60.)

Return to the lineup.

TIP | FORWARD MOVEMENT, FORWARD TRANSITIONS

It's not surprising that well-trained Equitation horses can tend to lose their forward impulsion. They have seen just about every kind of show ring and pattern imaginable. They have performed so many transitions that they start to function robotically, and the zip, energy, and gusto go out of their performance. Although it is nice to see a quiet, calm performance, if it starts to become lifeless and monotonous, then it seems as though the rider isn't really doing anything anymore; the horse is just on automatic pilot.

To prevent burnout in your horse and to restore forward movement, try some of the following:

- Do some trail riding.
- Gallop through a pasture.
- Include dressage in your training program.
- Begin jumping.
- At home practice patterns with lots of extended trot, extended canter, and gallop.
- Incorporate a lot of posting trot work in your at-home routines.

D **C** **B** **A**

A Rein back to cone B

B 180-degree turn on the
forehand right

Canter right lead

C Trot right diagonal

D Halt square

Stand for 3 seconds

Walk

Find a place on rail

PATTERN HELP

When a pattern starts with a rein back, you will move along in the lineup until it is your time to begin. You have the option of either facing forward until the judge gives you the nod to begin and then getting into position (using a combination of either a turn on the haunches or forehand with a sidepass) or of being in position when he gives you the nod. If you are facing backward, it will be awkward to twist around and watch the judge so it's usually better to stay facing forward and make your orientation switch smoothly just before you start your pattern.

A Rein back to cone B. (See Tip at right.)

B 180-degree turn on the forehand right. Give your horse enough room so that he doesn't hit the cone with his hind feet. If you make a line close to the cone, you will either have to rein back so that your horse's nose is one full horse length past the cone or you'll have to try to squeeze the turn on the forehand in between cone A and B, neither of which is the intention of the pattern. The best way to ride this pattern is to make your entire line far enough away from the cones (5 feet [1.5 m]) so that you can perform at the cones without running into any.

The aids for a turn on the forehand right are:

★ Flex the horse's head to the right with a shortened right rein.

★ Use a left supporting rein to limit right bend and to prevent the horse from walking forward out of the turn.

★ Keep your weight centered.

★ Use your right leg actively behind the girth to push the haunches to the left.

★ Use your left leg at the girth to keep the horse moving forward in a walk rhythm and to keep him from rushing sideways or backing up.

Canter right lead. (See Pattern 95.)

C Trot right diagonal. (See Pattern 57.)

D Halt square. (See Pattern 71.)

Stand for 3 seconds. (See Pattern 70.)

Walk. (See Pattern 60.)

Find a place on the rail.

Note: A pattern like this might have no cones at all, or the cones might be set outside the arena.

TIP FINISHING THE REIN BACK

When you need to perform another maneuver after a rein back, you don't want to finish the rein back with the horse's legs sprawled out behind him, as this would make it difficult for you to organize the horse to perform the next maneuver. You can just *hope* things work out, or you can plan so they do work out.

Decrease your aids 1 step before you are finished reining back so that the horse won't be in the middle of a large step back when you want to begin the turn. Finishing the rein back in a square position will put you in a better position to prepare for your 180-degree turn on the forehand.

PATTERN **74**

A Trot left diagonal

B Canter right lead circle

C Simple change through
   2 steps of trot

D Canter left lead

E Halt

   Rein back 4 steps

   Walk on the buckle

   Join new lineup

PATTERN HELP

A **Trot left diagonal.** (See Pattern 59.)

B **Canter right lead.** (See Pattern 55.)

Canter circle. Since there is no cone across from cone B to indicate diameter, the size is up to you.

C **Simple change through 2 steps of trot.** The simple change occurs at an imaginary point. There is no cone at C. There is enough room between cones B and D for you to canter 1 stride straight on the right lead, trot 1 stride (2 steps), and canter 1 stride straight on the left lead. (See Patterns 65 and 68.)

D **Canter left lead.** (See Pattern 55.)

E **Halt.** (See Pattern 59.)

Rein back 4 steps. (See Pattern 58.)

Walk on the buckle. As soon as you are finished backing, drop the reins so that the buckle is sitting just in front of the horse's withers. You should still retain control of the rein by holding the buckle with the fingers of one hand. It is optional which hand you use. This is similar to "walk on a long rein" in Dressage. It is to show that after a canter, halt, and rein back, your horse will walk off quietly without being "held." When the judging is complete (black arrow at left) you can pick up the reins and reestablish contact so you can maneuver into the lineup.

Join the new lineup.

TIP | **MEASURING STEPS AT THE TROT**

The trot is a 2-beat diagonal gait, so each stride has 2 steps. The left front and right hind take a step together, and the right front and left hind take a step together. You can count by feel or by looking. To count by looking, glance down at your horse's shoulders (don't lower your head or it will throw your balance forward) and watch them while you are trotting. Each time the left shoulder reaches forward, that is 1 stride. Learn to feel when your horse steps so that you can apply your aids without looking.

PATTERN 75*

Suitable for AHSA Saddle Seat 11 and Under 14

A Canter left lead

B Halt
Walk
Canter right lead

C Halt
Walk
Canter left lead

D Trot

E Halt

PATTERN HELP

A   Canter left lead. When this line curves to the right before cone B, you will be performing a counter-canter. (See Patterns 66 and 82.)

B   Halt. (See Pattern 59.)

Walk. (See Pattern 60.)

Canter right lead. You will be counter-cantering again before cone C. (See Patterns 63 and 82.)

C   Halt. (See Pattern 59.)

Walk. (See Pattern 60.)

Canter left lead. (See Pattern 63.)

D   Trot. (See Pattern 57.)

E   Halt. (See Pattern 54.)

Note: This pattern does not contain a rein back, so it will be called for later. (See Pattern 69.)

TIP   PREVENTING ANTICIPATION

When a horse anticipates, he often performs what he expects you will be asking for next. He has made an association in his mind that after point X, there usually is point Y, so he just shifts into automatic pilot. Although you might think it's cute the first few times your horse "reads your mind," it won't take long before you realize that it is very difficult to control a horse that anticipates. It's better if you keep your horse guessing. At home, practice a wide variety of maneuvers.

In this pattern there are several areas where your horse might think he knows what you want him to do. Between cones A and B and between cones B and C, he might think that since you are switching bend, you want him to switch leads. He might perform a flying lead change or just break down into a trot. (For more help, see Pattern 100.) At home, work on the counter-canter.

At cones B and C, after you halt, your horse might automatically start backing up. At home you must frequently halt and stand or halt and then quickly walk, trot, or canter forward.

At cone D, since you have halted twice from a canter already in the pattern, your horse might anticipate that you would halt from the third canter. You will need to apply strong forward driving aids so that you get a good posting trot out of the third canter.

Walk to cone A

A   Canter right lead

B   Halt

      270-degree turn on the
        forehand left

      Canter left lead

B   Trot

A   Halt

      Rein back 5 steps

      Find a place on rail

PATTERN HELP

Walk to cone A. (See Pattern 60.)

A Canter right lead. Be sure you canter from a walk, not from a halt. (See Pattern 63.)

B Halt. (Pattern 59)

270-degree turn on the forehand left. (See Tip at right and Patterns 77, 79, and 97.)

Canter left lead. (See Pattern 97.)

B Trot. (See Pattern 57.)

A Halt. (See Pattern 54.)

Rein back 5 steps. When you have finished reining back, the pattern is complete, so you can walk, trot, or canter to a place on the rail. A walk might take too long and interfere with the judge's line of vision or the next rider. Use a trot or canter to get to the rail, then break down to a walk or trot as you ease into position. (See Pattern 58.)

Find a place on the rail.

TIP FOOTFALL PATTERN OF TURN ON FOREHAND LEFT

The footfall pattern of the turn on the forehand is the same as the walk: left hind, left front, right hind, right front. In a turn on the forehand left, the pivot point is the left front foot. The left front remains relatively stationary, lifting up and setting down, but not swiveling, in place. The right front walks a small forward circle around the left front. The hind legs walk a half circle around the front legs. The left hind crosses over and in front of the right hind. The right hind uncrosses.

C

B

A

A Canter right lead

B Simple lead change

C Halt

Rein back 4 steps

360-degree turn on the
forehand left

Walk

Join new lineup

Pattern Help

A Canter right lead. (See Pattern 66.)

B Simple lead change. It is not specified whether the change is to be made from a walk, trot, or halt, and therefore the number of steps or strides is not specified. Choose the transition that your horse makes the smoothest to showcase your skills. (See Pattern 65.)

C Halt. (See Pattern 59.)

Rein back 4 steps. (See Pattern 58.)

360-degree turn on the forehand left. After the 360-degree turn, you should be facing the short end of the arena on the pattern line. Pause. You could walk straight forward and then turn to the left. But the pattern requests a walk on a diagonal line toward the new lineup. To connect up with that diagonal walk line, you should perform a 45-degree turn (either on the forehand or haunches) or an arcing turn. Whichever you choose, make it look deliberate, not haphazard. (See Tip at right.)

Walk.

Join the new lineup.

Note: This pattern does not contain a trot, so expect rail work in at least one direction.

TIP | **360-Degree Turn to the Left**

Whenever you perform a turn on the forehand greater than 180 degrees, you run the risk of overcurling your horse up front. What this means is that most horses are energetic about moving away from your leg and crossing over behind for about 90 or 180 degrees. After that you must use a more effective leg and avoid using more rein. The temptation is to pull the front end around when the horse stalls, but that's the opposite of what you want to do. You need to give the hind end a boost to keep it moving. All of this should be done at a 4-beat walk time, so before you hit 180 degrees, intensify your aids and keep the horse's front end as straight as possible.

PATTERN 78

A Trot left diagonal

Change diagonals

B Turn

X Halt

Turn on the forehand
180 degrees right

Canter right lead circle

X Halt

Turn on the haunches
180 degrees right

Canter right lead circle

Canter through **X**

Walk

Return to lineup

PATTERN HELP

A Trot left diagonal. (See Pattern 59.)

Change diagonals. (See Pattern 53.)

B Turn. (See Patterns 54 and 56.)

X Halt. X is an imaginary spot with no cone. Make X equidistant from cones C and D and in a direct line from the judge to cone B. (Some judges might place a cone directly across from cone B and stand in a different position to judge.)

Turn on the forehand 180 degrees right. Have the forehand turn aids clearly in mind so your horse is not confused when you ask for a turn on the haunches in a moment. (See Pattern 73.)

Canter right lead circle between point X and cone C. (See Pattern 95.)

X Halt. (See Pattern 59.)

Turn on the haunches 180 degrees right. Be sure your aids are very distinct or you might end up with a turn on the forehand or middle. (See Tip at right.)

Canter right lead circle between point X and cone D. (See Pattern 51.)

Canter through point X.

Walk. (See Pattern 67.)

Return to the lineup.

TIP 180-DEGREE TURN ON THE HAUNCHES RIGHT

From a halt, keep the horse's body straight, but flex his head at the throatlatch slightly to the right with a right direct rein. If you overbend the horse, he will likely move his haunches to the left as you turn. Use your left rein as a supporting rein to prevent overbending and to send weight diagonally to the right hind leg. Weight your right seat bone, and move your right shoulder back. This helps to plant the right hind leg, which is the pivot point of the turn. Let your left shoulder rotate forward as you turn, and use both reins to settle the weight on the horse's haunches. Use your left leg at the girth as a sideways driving aid to move the forehand to the right. You might need to use your leg slightly behind the girth.

Problems? If the horse steps to the left with his haunches, you are likely using too much right rein. Diminish right rein and keep your left leg behind the girth to prevent the haunches from stepping left.

B

A

A Sitting trot 3 strides

Pick up left diagonal posting

B Halt

90-degree turn on the
forehand left

Canter left lead

C Halt

Rein back 4 steps

90-degree turn on the
forehand right

Walk

Find a place on rail

C

© 1999 Cherry Hill *101 Horsemanship & Equitation Patterns*

PATTERN HELP

A Sitting trot 3 strides. (See Tip at right and Pattern 59.)

Then pick up left diagonal posting. (See Pattern 52.)

B Halt. (See Pattern 54.)

90-degree turn on the forehand left. The aids for a turn on the forehand left are:

★ Flex the horse's head to the left with a shortened left direct rein.

★ Support the left direct rein with a right supporting rein to prevent overbending and to prevent the horse from walking forward.

★ Keep your weight centered.

★ Use your left leg actively behind the girth to push the haunches to the right.

★ Use your right leg at the girth to keep the horse moving forward in a walk rhythm and to keep him from rushing sideways or backing up.

For the turn on the forehand left, you are moving the horse's haunches to the right, which is part of the pre-positioning canter aids. As you are finishing up the turn, be sure you have the horse's neck and head straight, not bent to the left. In fact, use a little more right rein to keep the horse up on his right shoulder before you ask for the canter left lead.

Canter left lead. (See Pattern 97.)

C Halt. (See Pattern 59.)

Rein back 4 steps. (See Pattern 58.

90-degree turn on the forehand right. (See Pattern 83.)

Walk. (See Pattern 60.)

Find a place on the rail.

TIP SITTING TROT

To sit the trot, you must be relaxed and balanced and connected to your horse. Regulate your breathing. Position your seat bones so that they are directly underneath you, not rolled in front of you or squashed out behind. Be sure your upper body is directly over your seat bones so that your shoulders are over your hips. If you lean your upper body back, it will roll your seat bones too far forward and cause your legs to swing out ahead of you, making you less stable. Keep your lower back straight, not hollow, and support it with strength from your abdominal muscles. Be sure you are not pinching with your legs or it could push you right up out of the saddle. Periodically, open your thighs so that they fall vertically along your horse's sides; this will let your seat bones drop even more deeply into the saddle.

PATTERN 80

Without stirrups:

A Trot right diagonal

B Canter left lead circle

C Halt

  Rein back 4 steps

  Walk

  Join new lineup

Pattern Help

This entire pattern is to be ridden without stirrups. (See Tip at right for more information.)

A Trot right diagonal. (See Pattern 59.)

B Canter left lead. (See Pattern 55.)

Canter circle. Since there is no cone across from cone B, the size of the circle is your option. A smaller circle shows more collection and a higher level of training, but a smaller circle ridden poorly is much worse than a larger circle ridden in top form. Choose a size that allows your horse to keep an even rhythm and bend throughout. (See Pattern 51.)

C Halt. (See Pattern 59.)

Rein back 4 steps. After the rein back, you can make an arcing turn or a 45-degree turn on the haunches or forehand to get on the diagonal walk line. (See Pattern 58.)

Walk. (See Pattern 60.)

Join the new lineup.

TIP RIDING WITHOUT STIRRUPS

At most shows, it is permissible for the judge to require the riders to perform any portion of a pattern or the entire pattern without stirrups. When you are asked to perform without irons, you can either leave the stirrup leathers down or cross them in front of your horse's withers. For safety's sake and to keep your horse free from distraction, it is best to cross the leathers in front of the horse's withers so that the left iron hangs on the right side of the horse's withers and the right iron hangs on the left side of the horse's withers.

When you ride the posting trot without stirrups, the judge is determining if you post correctly from the thigh and knee, not the stirrup tread. The idea is to assess your balance and correctness; it is not meant to be an endurance and fitness test.

Riding without stirrups should be just like riding with stirrups. You push both seat bones forward and squeeze with both legs while restraining the horse slightly with the bridle so that he doesn't trot or canter too fast. Don't be tempted to grip with your legs as you trot or canter; this will just make your horse move faster and push you up out of the saddle, making it harder for you to post or sit properly. The best practice for riding without stirrups is to ride bareback, but you also need to practice riding in your saddle with your feet out of the stirrups.

*Suitable for AHSA Hunter Seat Under 14

B

A

A Hand gallop

B Halt for 3 seconds

Trot to **X**

X Canter right circle

X Simple change

X Canter left circle

X Sitting trot to judge

Halt

Answer questions

PATTERN HELP

A Hand gallop. The hand gallop is an extended canter, which shows a marked increase in stride length over the canter without an increase in rhythm. The legs don't move quicker, but the legs do reach farther, resulting in a longer, more ground-covering stride. The hand gallop is called for in Hunter Seat Equitation and is ridden in two-point position in which your upper body is 30 degrees in front of the vertical. In the two-point position, the top part of your pelvis tilts forward, lifting your weight off the horse's back and transferring it forward to your legs. Your hands should be forward, up the horse's crest but not resting on the horse's neck.

B Halt for 3 seconds. (See Patterns 70 and 84.)

Trot to X. After cone B, you have an almost freestyle trot because there are no cones to denote point **X** or the size of the circles. If the judge is standing as in the drawing, then you can use her as a reference point. (See Pattern 59.)

X Canter right circle. (See Pattern 55.)

X Simple change. (See Pattern 65.)

X Canter left circle. (See Pattern 51.)

X Sitting trot to judge. (See Pattern 79.)

Halt. (See Pattern 54.)

Answer questions. (See Tip at right.)

Note: There is no rein back in this pattern, so the judge will ask for it later. When a pattern ends right at a judge, be ready to answer questions, address the reins, drop and pick up your irons, rein back and perform other fun surprises.

TIP ANSWERING QUESTIONS

It used to be much more common to ask Equitation riders questions about tack, horse anatomy, or riding than it is today. Most of this stems from the time constraints of a horse show. If you are asked a question by a judge, give a concise, polite reply. It's best if you know the right answer, but it is not the end of the world if you don't. If the judge asks, "Where are the panels?" and you point to your saddle and say, "They are the stuffing located on the underside of my saddle," that would be a sufficient and correct answer. If you don't know for sure, you might say, "They are part of the construction of my saddle, but I'm not sure exactly where they are located." If you give an incorrect answer, the judge will penalize accordingly.

Suitable for AHSA Hunter Seat Not to Jump, 14 to 18

B

A

C

A Canter right lead

B Counter-canter

C Halt

360-degree turn on the
forehand left

Halt

Dismount and mount

Pattern Help

A Canter right lead. (See Pattern 66.)

B Counter-canter around the corner. The counter-canter is a deliberate, balanced canter on one lead while the horse is traveling in a curve in the opposite direction. When you are cantering on the right lead and ask a horse to take a left turn, you are asking him to counter-canter. When counter-cantering, there should be no change in rhythm or stride, and the horse should be bent toward the lead. When a horse can canter on the lead opposite to the direction of travel, he is exhibiting great training, balance, and strength. It is a maneuver that shows whether a horse is just performing robotically or if the rider is effectively riding the horse. (See Pattern 96.)

C Halt. (See Pattern 59.)

360-degree turn on the forehand left. (See Pattern 77.)

Halt. (See Pattern 71.)

Dismount and mount. (See Tip at right.)

Note: This pattern does not contain a trot, walk, or rein back, so expect rail work in at least one direction. (See Pattern 69.)

TIP DISMOUNTING AND MOUNTING

To dismount, you can either slide down or vault off. To slide down, remove your right foot from the iron; place your left hand, holding the reins, on the horse's withers, with your right hand on the pommel; tilt your upper body slightly forward as you swing your right leg over the horse's back; then drop the left iron and slide down close to the horse facing the horse's side.

To vault off, proceed as above except remove both feet from the irons. When you swing your leg over the horse, you swivel on your crotch until your body is facing your horse's near side. Then give a light push off so that you land a little farther away from the horse but facing his side just like the slide down method.

After dismount, it is correct to draw the reins over the horse's head and stand next to the horse facing forward. However, in the interest of time, the judge may tell you to remount immediately.

To mount, take up the reins in your left hand and place that hand on the withers. Face the horse's haunches. Grasp the near iron with your right hand, turn it toward you, and insert your left foot into the iron. Turn the toe of your boot into the girth so you won't press into the horse's skin as you mount. Use your right hand to grasp either the off pommel or the cantle. Beware that if you try to pull yourself up with your right hand on the cantle, you might pull the saddle off to the near side. And you have to move your right arm just as you are swinging up. Learn to place your right hand on the off pommel, so you can pull against the withers and keep your hand in position during the entire mounting. Step up or bounce once or twice on your right foot. Rise and swing your right leg over the horse's back and mount. Lower yourself softly into the saddle; don't land with a thud. Find the right iron by feel with your boot, not by looking for it.

The judge will take the size of the rider into consideration when evaluating mounting and dismounting.

A Trot left diagonal

B Halt

　90-degree turn on the
　forehand right

　Walk 2 strides

　90-degree turn on the
　forehand left

　Trot right diagonal

C Halt

　Rein back 4 steps

　Canter right circle

D End of pattern

　Return to lineup at any gait

D

C

B

A

Pattern Help

A **Trot left diagonal.** (See Pattern 59.)

B **Halt.** (See Pattern 54.)

90-degree turn on the forehand right. (See Tip at right.)

Walk 2 strides. The space between cones B and C should be about 6 feet (1.8 m) to accommodate 2 strides of walk. If you have to make a choice between exactly 2 strides of walk and staying on the straight line to cone C, opt for the straight line to cone C. (See Patterns 56 and 60.)

90-degree turn on the forehand left. (See Pattern 79.)

Trot right diagonal. (See Pattern 59.)

C **Halt.** (See Pattern 54.)

Rein back 4 steps. (See Pattern 58.)

Canter right circle. (See Patterns 51, 66, and 73.)

D **End of pattern.** You canter straight through cone D, keeping an even pace. After cone D, you can continue cantering toward the lineup as long as it doesn't disrupt the next exhibitor.

Return to the lineup at any gait.

TIP 90-Degree Turn on the Forehand Right

Give your horse enough room so that he doesn't hit cone B with his hind feet as you turn. (See Pattern 73 for more on this.) Make your entire line far enough away from the cones (5 feet [1.5 m]) so that you can perform at the cones without running into any.

The aids for a turn on the forehand right are:

- Flex the horse's head to the right with a shortened right direct rein.
- Support the right direct rein with a left supporting rein to prevent overbending and to prevent the horse from walking forward.
- Keep your weight centered.
- Use your right leg actively behind the girth to push the haunches to the left.
- Use your left leg at the girth to keep the horse moving forward in a walk rhythm and to keep him from rushing sideways or backing up.

PATTERN 84

A Trot 2 strides

Extend the trot

B Halt

90-degree turn on the forehand left

Canter left lead 1 stride

Hand gallop

C Halt

Rein back 4 steps

Sitting trot

PATTERN HELP

A Trot 2 strides. (See Patterns 56 and 59.)

Extend the trot. (See Tip at right.) After the extension, bring your horse back to a regular trot for at least 1 stride before the halt.

B Halt. (See Pattern 54.)

90-degree turn on the forehand left. (See Pattern 79.)

Canter left lead 1 stride. (See Patterns 66 and 97.)

Hand gallop. (See Pattern 81.)

C Halt. The halt should be performed promptly but smoothly. The horse should stop with his hind legs under his body, not out behind with the front brakes jammed! To accomplish this, about 2 to 3 strides before cone C, go from your two-point position of the hand gallop back to your regular seat for the canter. Gather your horse and reestablish contact through your seat, legs, and hands. When you ask for the halt, use the same aids as you would for canter to halt (see Pattern 59); your aim is a square halt without roughness.

Rein back 4 steps. (See Pattern 58.)

Sitting trot. (See Pattern 79.)

Pattern ends after 3 to 4 strides of sitting trot.

TIP EXTENDED TROT

The extended trot is at the same tempo as the regular trot, but the horse moves with longer strides, pushing and driving with his haunches. The extended trot has great impulsion and the horse reaches farther forward with his front legs. Because the extended trot has the longest moment of suspension, it covers the most ground. The hind hooves should overstep the front prints by a considerable distance. There is a distinct lengthening of the horse's frame with the nose stretching forward and somewhat down.

To post the extended trot, drive with your seat each time you prepare to rise. Squeeze with your legs each time you prepare to rise. Keep your hands low, especially your outside hand, to encourage your horse to reach long and low.

To sit the extended trot, drive with your seat and squeeze with your legs. Keep your upper body vertical with your shoulders slightly back, tighten your abdominal muscles, and keep your hands low and somewhat giving to encourage the horse to move forward.

C

B

A

D

E

A Walk

B Sidepass

C Canter left lead

E Halt

180-degree turn on the forehand right

Canter right lead

D Trot

C Halt

Rein back 4 steps

Pattern Help

A Walk. Don't necessarily go to a halt before the sidepass; it's better for forward movement of the sidepass if you don't. (See Pattern 60.)

B Sidepass. (See Tip at right.)

C Canter left lead. The sidepass right is a natural setup for a left lead canter depart. It is not necessary to come to a halt before you canter; in fact it's preferable if you don't. (See Pattern 66.)

E Halt. (See Pattern 59.)

180-degree turn on the forehand right. (See Pattern 73.)

Canter right lead. (See Pattern 95.)

D Trot. Although it is not designated what diagonal you should be on, the judge will expect you to know that, since you are turning right, you should be on the left diagonal. (See Pattern 57.)

C Halt. (See Pattern 54.)

Rein back 4 steps. (See Pattern 58.)

TIP SIDEPASS

You can ride a sidepass with your horse straight (best in this situation), counter-flexed (easiest for first training a horse), or flexed into the direction of the sidepass (most difficult). In all cases, the seat and leg aids and footfall patterns are the same. Only the rein aids are different.

For a sidepass to the right, the footfall sequence is the same as the 4-beat walk; the action is as follows:

1. Left hind crosses over in front of the right hind.
2. Left front crosses over in front of the right front.
3. Right hind uncrosses from behind the left hind and steps to the right.
4. Right front uncrosses from behind the left front and steps to the right.

Steps 2 and 3 happen almost in unison, allowing the horse to retain his balance.

To sidepass right:

- Weight your left seat bone.
- Apply your left leg at or behind the girth and use it in rhythm with the lifting of the left hind leg; this is a sideways driving aid.
- Keep your right leg on the horse, but very lightly; do not take your leg off and allow daylight between your leg and the horse's side.
- Use slightly more left direct rein and a right supporting rein to keep the horse's head and neck straight.

A Rein back

B 180-degree turn on the forehand right

Canter right lead

C Simple change through 1 stride of trot

Left lead circle

Trot

D Extend the trot

E Halt

PATTERN HELP

A   Rein back. (See Pattern 73.)

B   180-degree turn on the forehand right. In this turn, your predominant aid is your right leg driving the horse's haunches to the left. This puts the haunches in an advantageous pre-canter position for a right lead. Be sure you maintain a good contact with the left rein throughout the turn and especially toward the end to prevent overbending and to keep the horse's weight up on his left side. Then the canter aids for right lead can be applied. (See Pattern 73.)

Canter right lead. (See Pattern 95.)

C   Simple change through 1 stride of trot. (See Patterns 65 and 68.)

Left lead circle. (See Pattern 51.)

Trot upon completion of circle. You will want to trot promptly at the circle juncture so that you can establish the contact, rhythm, and frame of the trot before you extend at cone D. (See Pattern 57.)

D   Extend the trot. Post the extended trot. You will be expected to know that it is not correct to perform a transition from extended trot to a halt. You must fit in 1 to 2 strides of regular trot before you halt. This leaves you even less room for your extension, so you must start your extension as soon after the circle as possible to make the most use of your space. (See Pattern 84.)

E   Halt. (See Pattern 54.)

Note: This pattern has no walk, so expect rail work in at least one direction or the judge to add it to the end of the pattern.

TIP | POLISH

There is nothing extremely difficult in this pattern. It contains everyday intermediate gaits and movements in a fairly simple line pattern. When a pattern like this is posted, it can be easy to look at it too casually, but don't — this could lead to errors. Instead, view this pattern as a time to shine. Polish up your performance and show your finesse. Work on making the back, turn, and canter a continuous flow of aids that makes it seem like an effortless dance routine. Make the simple change the next best thing to a flying change. Draw a perfect Michelangelo circle with your horse's hooves. Make your trot–extended trot–trot so elastic that the judge will wonder if you are riding a rubber band! Ride from your seat and use rein cues so subtle that the judge can't even detect them. Remember, it's better to perform simple things well than more advanced things in poor form.

Advanced English Equitation Patterns

Advanced level riders use subtle aids to produce consistent, fluid performances. Advanced Equitation patterns include everything in beginning and intermediate patterns plus flying lead changes, 360-degree turns on the haunches or forehand, rein back and turn, counter-canter, and other movements.

On the following page, you'll find four blank arenas where you can record patterns that you've ridden at shows.

TRAINING NOTES
_____
_____
_____
_____
_____
_____
_____
_____
_____
_____
_____
_____
_____
_____
_____
_____
_____
_____
_____
_____
_____
_____
_____
_____
_____
_____

COMPETITION GOALS
_____
_____
_____
_____
_____
_____
_____
_____
_____
_____
_____
_____
_____
_____
_____
_____
_____
_____
_____
_____
_____
_____
_____
_____
_____
_____

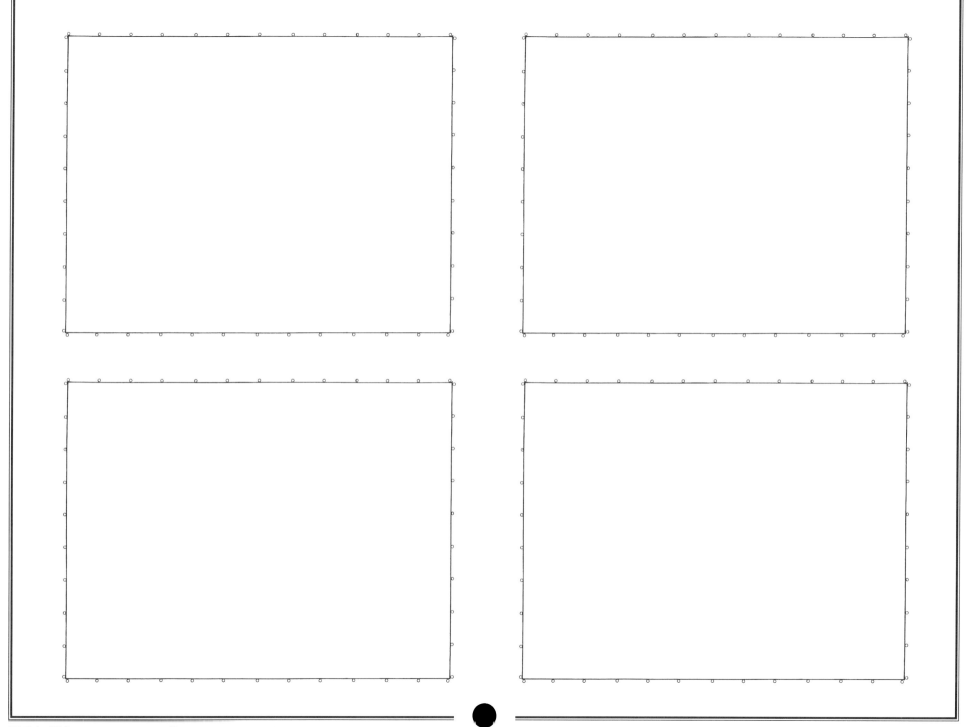

C

B

A

A Trot right diagonal

B Halt

270-degree turn on
the forehand right

Canter left lead

Hand gallop

C Halt

Rein back 4 steps

Walk

Find a position on rail

PATTERN HELP

A Trot right diagonal. (See Pattern 59.)

B Halt. (See Pattern 54.)

270-degree turn on the forehand right. In this ¾ turn, the horse is bent slightly right and you use your right leg to move the horse's haunches to the left. (See Tip at right and Pattern 73.)

Canter left lead. (See Tip at right.)

Then hand gallop in two-point position. (See Pattern 81.)

C Halt. (See Pattern 84.)

Rein back 4 steps. (See Pattern 58.)

After the rein back and before the walk, you can just walk straight ahead; if you are looking for some extra credit, though, you can perform a 60-degree turn on the haunches right (see Pattern 78) to get you lined up with the walk line as drawn.

Walk. (See Pattern 60.)

Find a position on the rail.

TIP CHOICES IN PRE-CANTER POSITIONING

When a turn on the forehand right is followed by a canter left lead, or a turn on the forehand left is followed by a canter right lead, the horse does not finish the turn in an advantageous pre-canter position. In a turn right followed by a canter left, you have two choices for your canter depart. First, as you finish the turn, you can straighten your horse, apply the pre-canter positioning aids, which will shift the horse's weight off to the right, and then apply the canter aids (this is how you have been riding canter departs and simple changes). Alternatively, if you and your horse are very well practiced and confident, you can go directly from the turn on the forehand right. Just as you are finishing up the turn, you'd straighten the horse's head and neck, drive with your right seat bone and leg, and then add a little left flexion. Your canter line will be a few feet to the left of the canter line in the first method. This method could backfire on you if you are not practiced and your horse is not very well schooled.

Walk to cone A

A Trot

B Change diagonals

C Change diagonals

D Halt

Rein back 4 steps

Canter left lead

E Simple change through
1 stride of trot

F Halt

Walk

Find a position
on rail

PATTERN HELP

As you prepare for the pattern, you can sidepass your horse to the left until you are about 20 feet (6.1 m) from cone A. When it is your turn to work the pattern, make an arcing turn to the left and walk straight to cone A.

Note: The cones in this pattern will always be on your right except for the halt at cone D.

Walk to cone A. (See Pattern 60.)

A Trot. Post on the left diagonal since you are turning right. (See Pattern 56.)

B Change diagonals. When your shoulder passes cone B, sit 2 beats and post on the right diagonal since you will be turning left. This loop of the serpentine is narrow because it is *between* two cones. You will have to use extra left leg, left seat bone, and left rein. (See Pattern 53.)

C Change diagonals. When your shoulder passes cone C, sit 2 beats and post on the left diagonal.

D Halt. (See Pattern 54.)

Rein back 4 steps. (See Pattern 58.)

Canter left lead. (See Patterns 73 and 99; see first tip at right.)

E Simple change through 1 stride of trot to right lead. (See Pattern 68.)

F Halt. (See Pattern 59.)

Walk. (See Pattern 60.)

Find a place on the rail.

Note: This is a very time-consuming pattern that might be used at a schooling show, a small show or in a medal class. Since the exhibitor has exhibited the walk, trot on both diagonals, canter on both leads, and rein back, rail work might not be required.

TIP QUESTION?

When you see a pattern like this and have a question, don't be afraid to ask. If it is unclear to you whether you should go straight forward after the rein back at D and canter with the cone on your *left* or canter at a slight angle as drawn, with the cone on your right, ask the judge for clarification.

TIP SERPENTINE SHAPE

A serpentine is a series of half circles connected by straight lines. Each loop should be equal in length and width to the other loops. In this pattern, one loop has purposely been made narrower and one made wider to accommodate the test and to evaluate the flexibility of the horse and rider team.

The secret to riding shapely serpentines is to use your eyes to plan a serpentine as half circles connected by straight lines rather than a wiggly line that goes up and down the arena. As you ride one of the half circles, when you end the bend, you should be perpendicular to the long side of the arena.

F

D

B

A

E

C

A Trot left diagonal and drop irons

B Change diagonals

C Canter left lead and pick up irons

D Halt

360-degree turn on the forehand right

E Canter right lead

F Halt

Rein back 4 steps

Walk

Join new lineup

PATTERN HELP

A Trot left diagonal and drop irons. The intention here is to test your ability to drop the stirrup irons while in motion. As soon as you begin posting, remove your feet from the irons with as little a movement as possible. Let the irons dangle as you continue with the pattern. (See Tip at right and Pattern 59.)

B Change diagonals. Sit 2 beats, pick up the right diagonal, and trot the first half of the circle. (See Pattern 53.)

C Canter left lead and pick up irons. After the canter depart, pick up the irons without looking. At the canter, the irons will probably be softly banging on the front of the ankles of your boot. You can just flex your knees and place your feet in the irons. If you are having trouble finding one or both of the irons, you can wait until you halt, but you will lose points as the test was to be during motion. (See Tip at right and Pattern 55.)

D Halt. (See Pattern 59.)

360-degree turn on the forehand right. Give your horse enough room so when you are completing the second half of the turn, his haunches don't hit the cone. Push your horse's haunches to the left with your right leg, which is part of the pre-canter positioning aid. You must take care to keep the weight of the horse's forehand over to the left as well, by judicious use of the left supporting rein as you finish the 360-degree turn. (See Pattern 93.)

E Canter right lead. There is no cone at position E. It is an imaginary point just after cone D. (See Pattern 95.)

F Halt. (See Pattern 59.)

Rein back 4 steps. (See Pattern 58.)

Walk. (See Pattern 60.)

Join the new lineup.

TIP | **DROPPING AND PICKING UP IRONS**

This test has a practical purpose. It is likely that you will at one time or another lose a stirrup iron when riding. Learning how to pick up an iron while your horse continues walking, jogging, or trotting requires some practice. First you have to break yourself of the habit of looking down as most people do to visually locate the stirrup iron. When you look down, you have lost control of the horse because you are no longer looking where you are going. Also if you look over in front of your leg and down, you are off balance to the front and one side and could easily fall off. The best way to regain a lost stirrup iron is to sit balanced in the center of the horse and locate the iron by feel.

PATTERN 90

A   Trot left diagonal
    Change diagonals
B   Turn left
C   Canter left lead circle
C   Flying lead change
E   Turn right
F   Halt
    360-degree turn on the
        forehand right
    Walk
    Join new lineup

PATTERN HELP

A Trot left diagonal. (See Pattern 59.)

Change diagonals. (See Pattern 53.)

B Turn left. (See Patterns 54 and 56.)

C Canter left lead. C is an imaginary point that should be halfway between cones B and F directly on the line between them. (See Pattern 55.)

Canter circle. (See Pattern 51.)

C Flying change to right lead. (See Tip at right.)

E Turn right. (See Pattern 68.)

F Halt. (See Pattern 59.)

360-degree turn on the forehand right. (See Pattern 93.)

Walk. (See Pattern 60.)

Join the new lineup.

TIP FLYING CHANGE TO RIGHT LEAD

A flying change consists of a three-point check, pre-positioning aids, and the lead change itself.

Three-Point Check. As you are preparing for a flying change from left to right, you need to check three things:

1. Be sure your horse is cantering a true 3-beat canter. If he is "4-beating," he won't have enough impulsion and his legs won't be in the right place at the right time for a change.
2. Be sure your horse's body is straight. It is much more difficult to get a clean, prompt lead change if your horse's spine is curved.
3. Be sure you feel contact with your horse through the reins. You should be able to further collect your horse by just moving your hands back an inch. And if you move your hand forward an inch, he should stretch forward.

Pre-positioning. Now, with your horse cantering on the left lead, move your hands over to the left. You are shifting the horse's weight to his left side much like you do for a canter depart. At the same time, put your right leg on the horse to shift his weight left. When you are cantering on the left lead, your left seat bone is more forward than your right seat bone. You can hold this pre-change positioning for 2 to 3 strides of canter if you want at home. At the show, you want to hone it down to 1 stride.

The Change. For the change, keep the horse straight and up on his left shoulder so that his right shoulder is "free" to change. Also, be sure you have contact to prevent a speedup during the change. Do this by maintaining contact with the left supporting rein.

Relax the pressure of your right leg that is holding the horse to the left (this "invites" the horse to the right), and move your right seat bone forward. Apply your left leg behind the girth to ask for the change just as you would for a canter depart.

After the horse makes the change, you can initiate the new bend.

B   **A**

C

D

A   Walk

     Extend the walk

B   Canter left lead

C   Flying change

D   Trot

C   Change diagonals

B   Halt

     Rein back 6 steps

     Find a place on rail

PATTERN HELP

A Walk. Be ready to go at cone A when the last exhibitor is finishing up. You will be walking 50 to 60 feet (15.3–18.3 m), which will take about 10 strides. (See Pattern 60.)

Extend the walk. Demonstrate a difference between the walk and the extended walk on the long walk line. Drive your horse forward with more energy from your seat to increase the reach of his hind legs. At the same time, give him room to stretch forward by giving him a slightly longer rein while still maintaining contact. Let your horse drop his head a little bit and reach forward to extend the movement of his forelegs.

B Canter left lead. Keep your horse straight as you ask for the canter depart; then ask for left bend. (See Pattern 63.)

C Flying change to right lead. (See Pattern 90.) The ideal change has an even pace with no speedup, kicking, bucking, or tail swishing. The change should take place as your shoulders pass cone C.

D Trot. The transition needs to be forward, and in advanced competition you will need to be posting on the correct (left) diagonal by the second beat. (See Pattern 57.)

C Change diagonals. Sit 2 beats on the 1 stride where your horse will be straight in the center of the figure 8. Then post on the right diagonal as you add left bend. (See Pattern 53.)

B Halt. (See Pattern 54.)

Rein back 6 steps. (See Tip below.)

Find a place on the rail. After the rein back, get to the rail in an expedient manner, either at the trot or canter.

TIP PREVENTING LOCKUP ON A REIN BACK

The key to preventing lockup during a rein back is to have a good starting point. At the beginning of a rein back, adhere to the following criteria:

- The horse is straight.
- You are sitting with equal weight on both seat bones.
- Your legs are both at the girth, passive at the moment.
- You have contact with the horse's mouth.
- The horse is rounding into the contact; that is, he is flexing vertically at the jaw, poll, and throatlatch; the topline of his neck is slightly arched; and his back is flat or raised.

Suitable for AHSA Saddle Seat Open and 14 and Over

A Canter left lead

B Halt

Canter right lead

C Halt and drop irons

Canter left lead

D Halt and pick up irons

Canter left lead

E Halt

Rein back 5 steps

Pattern Help

A **Canter left lead.** (See Pattern 66.)

B **Halt.** (See Pattern 59.)

   Canter right lead. Be careful that as you are positioning and then cantering your horse that you are not wagging his body back and forth across the line. If his haunches move one way and then the other, your aids are not correct and you are not ready for advanced competition. (See Patterns 62 and 66.)

C **Halt and drop irons.** Remove your feet from the stirrups for the next canter depart and halt. (See Patterns 59 and 89.)

   Canter left lead. (See Patterns 55 and 66.)

D **Halt and pick up irons.** Without looking down, find the irons with the toe of your boots and then flip them into position so that the ball of your foot is securely on the tread. (See Patterns 59 and 89.)

   Canter left lead. (See Pattern 66.)

E **Halt.** (See Pattern 59.)

   Rein back 5 steps. (See Pattern 58.)

Note: This pattern does not contain a walk or trot, so expect rail work in at least one direction.

TIP | **VISUALIZATION**

When you are faced with a pattern like this, it is often better to look at it as a series of simple changes through a halt rather than a group of canter-halt-canter transitions. Thinking of it as a series of simple changes keeps the forward motion aspect to it in your mind and body language, and you will likely communicate it to the horse that way.

D

C

B

A

A   Trot left diagonal

B   Canter right lead
       circle

B   Halt

       360-degree turn on
       the forehand right

       Canter left lead

C   Canter circle to left

D   Halt

       Rein back 4 steps

       Walk

       Join new lineup

PATTERN HELP

A Trot left diagonal. With the cone on your left, post on the left diagonal. As you approach cone B, sit 1 stride while the horse is still straight to position the horse for the canter. (See Pattern 59.)

B Canter right lead. After the depart, initiate right bend. (See Pattern 55.)

Canter circle to the right. (See Pattern 51.)

B Halt. (See Pattern 59.)

360-degree turn on the forehand right. Whenever you perform a turn on the forehand greater than 180 degrees, you run the risk of overcurling your horse's neck. Most horses are willing to move away from your leg and cross over behind for about 90 or 180 degrees. After that you must use a more effective right leg and left supporting rein and avoid using more right direct rein. The temptation is to pull the front end around when the horse freezes, but that just makes things worse. You need to give the hind end an extra boost to keep it moving. All of this should be done at a 4-beat walk time, so before you hit 180 degrees intensify your aids and keep the horse's front end as straight as possible.

Canter left lead. (See Pattern 87.)

C Canter circle to the left. With the cone on your right, make a circle to the left. (See Pattern 51.)

D Halt. (See Pattern 59.)

Rein back 4 steps. (See Pattern 58.)

Walk. (See Pattern 60.)

Join the new lineup.

TIP DEVELOPING FINESSE

There is nothing new in this pattern. It contains everything you have demonstrated up to this point. Now it is time to polish your performance and develop finesse. When you were a novice exhibitor, you might have over-aided your horse to ensure that he performed the prescribed movements at the right spot. When riding English, your rein aids should be very slight and not really noticeable. Because you ride with more contact than a Western rider does, you should have instantaneous communication with your horse's mouth, making large hand and rein movements unnecessary. Rein aids given outside an imaginary 4-inch (10.2 cm) square box in the vicinity of the horse's withers are unacceptable in English riding, and it would be best if you would confine your aids to a 2-inch (5.1 cm) square box.

Your goal should be to ride your horse primarily with your seat and legs. Use very subtle weight and leg cues for initiation of canter departs, bending, forehand turns, and reining back.

A Trot right diagonal

B Canter left lead

C Turn left

D Halt

　　360-degree turn on the
　　　forehand left

　　Canter right lead

E Halt

　　Rein back 4 steps

　　Walk

　　Return to lineup

PATTERN HELP

A Trot right diagonal. With the cone on your left, post on the right diagonal. A prompt departure will ensure you get 3 to 4 good strides in before cone B. (See Pattern 59.)

B Canter left lead. (See Pattern 55.)

C Turn left. With the cone on your left, make a concise turn without pulling your horse around with the left rein. (See Pattern 68.)

D Halt. With the cone on your right, halt when your shoulders are at cone D. (See Pattern 59.)

   360-degree turn on the forehand left. (See Pattern 77.)

   Canter right lead. (See Tip at right.)

E Halt. The cone is on your right. (See Pattern 59.)

   Rein back 4 steps. (See Pattern 58.)

   Walk. (See Pattern 60.)

   Return to the lineup.

TIP LEFT FOREHAND TURN TO RIGHT LEAD

When a turn on the forehand left is followed by a canter right lead, the horse does not finish the turn in an advantageous pre-canter position. You should finish the turn; then straighten your horse; apply the pre-canter positioning aids, which will shift the horse's weight off to the left; and then apply the canter aids for the right lead. This is how you have been riding canter departs and lead changes.

If you and your horse are very well practiced and confident, you can go directly into the right lead canter from the turn on the forehand left. Just as you are finishing up the turn, straighten the horse's head and neck, drive with your left seat bone and leg, and then add a little right flexion. Your canter line will be a few feet to the right of the canter line in the normal method. This "shortcut" method could backfire on you, however, if you are not practiced and your horse is not very well schooled.

B

A

C

D

F

G

A Trot left diagonal

Change diagonals

B Turn left

C Halt

180-degree turn on the
  forehand right

Canter right lead

Canter circle to the right

C Halt

180-degree turn on the
  haunches right

Walk

E Canter left lead

F Turn right, counter-cantering

G Halt

Rein back 4 steps

Join new lineup

Pattern Help

A Posting trot left diagonal. (See Pattern 56.)

Change diagonals. Sit 2 beats and change to the right diagonal before the corner at cone B. (See Pattern 53.)

B Turn left. (See Patterns 54 and 56.)

C Halt. C is an imaginary spot halfway between cones B and F and on a line directly between them. Be glad that there is no cone to crunch! (See Pattern 54.)

180-degree turn on the forehand right. (See Pattern 73.)

Canter right lead. (See Tip at right.)

Canter circle to the right. (See Pattern 51.)

C Halt. (See Pattern 59.)

180-degree turn on the haunches right. (See Pattern 78.)

Walk. (See Pattern 60.)

E Canter left lead. This is an imaginary spot halfway between cones C and F. (See Pattern 63.)

F Turn right, counter-cantering. (See Patterns 68, 82, and 96.)

G Halt. (See Pattern 59.)

Rein back 4 steps. (See Pattern 58.)

Join the new lineup.

TIP **RIGHT FOREHAND TURN TO RIGHT LEAD**

When you finish a turn on the forehand right, the horse's haunches are shifted over to the left side. This is good. It is a perfect pre-canter position for the canter right lead aids. However, the horse's forehand is bent slightly to the right, which weights the right shoulder. This is not so good because you want the horse's weight to be on the left shoulder *before* you apply canter right lead aids. By the way, it takes approximately 4 steps for a horse to complete a 180-degree forehand turn. Therefore, just as you are finishing up your forehand turn, during the third step apply more left supporting rein and release right bend so that your horse finishes the turn very straight. Then apply your canter right lead aids.

Walk to cone A

A   Canter left lead

B   Halt

    90-degree turn on the
      forehand right

    Counter-canter large
      right lead circle

B   Simple change through
      1 stride of trot

A   Halt

    Rein back 5 steps

    Find a place on rail

B   **A**

PATTERN HELP

Walk to cone A. (See Pattern 60.)

A Canter left lead. With the cone about 6 feet (1.8 m) to your left, canter a line toward cone B. (See Pattern 63.)

B Halt. With the cone about 6 feet (1.8m) to your left, halt. (See Pattern 59.)

90-degree turn on the forehand right. In a turn to the right, your horse's haunches will be moving to the left. That is why you needed to plan room to maneuver. (See Pattern 83.)

Counter-canter right lead. (See Tip at right and Pattern 82.)

Canter large circle.

B Simple change through 1 stride of trot to left lead. Note the cone is on your left. (See Patterns 65 and 68.)

A Halt. (See Pattern 59.)

Rein back 5 steps. (See Pattern 58.)

Find a place on the rail.

There is no trot in this pattern, so rail work in at least one direction will be required.

TIP COUNTER-CANTER ON A CIRCLE

The counter-canter is not a canter on the wrong lead around a circle. It is a controlled and balanced exercise that shows great muscle development and a high level of training.

When you canter right lead, your horse should have slight right bend. Your right seat bone should be ahead of your left seat bone. Weight should be deep in your right heel. Your right leg will be at the girth to keep horse slightly bent right. Your left leg will be behind the girth to maintain the right lead.

When you counter-canter a circle to the left on the right lead, you want to maintain the above aids. You want the horse to be looking slightly to the outside of the circle, but his body should be 100 percent on the track of the circle, not angled so his haunches drift in toward the center of the circle. Your rein aids will depend on the level of your horse's training but will generally be a slight right direct rein to create right flexion and a left supporting rein to prevent overbending. The goals of your rein aids are:

- To balance and direct the horse as he turns around the circle
- To keep him on the circle line
- To prevent the horse from overbending to the right

When counter-cantering:

- Keep your hips parallel to your horse's hips.
- Keep your shoulders parallel to your horse's shoulders.

E **D** **C** **B** **A**

A Rein back

B 180-degree turn on
the forehand left

Canter left lead

C Flying change

Canter straight 1 stride

Counter-canter left circle

Trot

D Extend trot

E Halt

PATTERN HELP

A Rein back. (See Patterns 58 and 73.)

B 180-degree turn on the forehand left. It will take approximately 4 steps for your horse to complete a 180-degree turn. The aids for a turn on the forehand left are:

★ Flex horse's head to the left with a shortened left direct rein.

★ Support the left direct rein with a right supporting rein to prevent overbending and to prevent the horse from walking forward.

★ Keep your weight centered.

★ Use your left leg actively behind the girth to push the haunches to the right.

★ Use your right leg at the girth to keep the horse moving forward in a walk rhythm and to keep him from rushing sideways or backing up.

Canter left lead. (See Tip at right.)

C Flying change to right lead. The change should take place when your shoulders pass cone C. (See Pattern 90.)

Canter straight 1 stride.

Then counter-canter circle to the left. (See Pattern 96.)

When circle is completed, trot. (See Pattern 57.)

D Extend the trot for a few strides, then trot. (See Pattern 84.)

E Halt. (See Pattern 54.)

Note: The cones are on your right throughout the pattern.

TIP | LEFT FOREHAND TURN TO LEFT LEAD

When you finish the turn on the forehand left, the horse's haunches are shifted over to the right side, which is good. It is a perfect pre-canter position for the canter left lead aids. However, the horse's forehand is bent slightly to the left, which weights the left shoulder. This is not so good because you want the horse's weight to be on the right shoulder *before* you apply canter left lead aids. Therefore, just as you are finishing up your forehand turn, during the third step apply more right supporting rein and release left bend so that your horse finishes the turn very straight. Then apply your canter left lead aids.

A Canter right lead

B Halt

Sidepass right

Canter left lead

C Halt

Rein back 4 steps

Sitting trot circle

Posting trot through
cone D on left diagonal

Return to lineup

D

C

B

A

PATTERN HELP

A **Canter right lead.** (See Pattern 66.)

B **Halt.** (See Pattern 59.)

Sidepass right. (See Pattern 85.)

Canter left lead. (See Patterns 66 and 85.)

C **Halt.** (See Pattern 59.)

Rein back 4 steps. (See Pattern 58.)

Sitting trot circle to the right. (See Tip at right and Pattern 79.)

When finished, posting trot through cone D on the left diagonal. (See Pattern 52.)

Return to lineup at the gait of your choice.

Note: Cones are on the left throughout this pattern. This pattern does not contain a walk, so expect rail work in at least one direction or the judge to add it to the end of the pattern.

TIP — **REIN BACK TO SITTING TROT**

The rein back to sitting trot transition is fun and springy. That's because you and your horse go from a diagonal gait in reverse to a diagonal gait forward. If a horse in on the bit and collected, you will feel like you are springing forward when your horse trots. You should just let your horse's weight begin to settle on the last rearward step when you transform the energy to the first forward trot step. Don't lean back when you are reining back because it might cause the horse to hollow his back and place his hind legs way behind his haunches. He needs his hind legs well underneath himself to spring forward into a prompt trot depart. Also, you don't want to be "left behind the action." This is designed to be rein back, spring forward, and trot. There should not be a halt or any walk steps in between.

A Walk

B 90-degree turn on the forehand left

Trot

C Canter left lead

D Hand gallop

C Simple change

B Halt

Rein back 6 steps

90-degree turn on the forehand left

Walk

Find a place on rail

PATTERN HELP

A Walk. (See Pattern 60.)

B 90-degree turn on the forehand left. Since your horse's haunches will be swinging to the right, you can be fairly close to cone B. (See Pattern 79.)

   Trot. Since you will be bending right, post on the left diagonal. (See Pattern 59.)

C Canter left lead. (See Pattern 55.)

D Hand gallop. Bring your horse down to a canter for 1 stride before the simple change to the right lead. (See Pattern 81.)

C Simple change. It is not specified whether it is to be through a walk, trot, or halt, nor is it specified how many steps or strides to use. Choose the configuration that showcases your skills. Do not perform a flying lead change. (See Pattern 68.)

B Halt. (See Pattern 59.)

   Rein back 6 steps. (See Pattern 101.)

   90-degree turn on the forehand left. (See Pattern 79.)

   Walk. (See Pattern 60.)

   Find a place on the rail.

TIP | **FINISHING THE REIN BACK IN GOOD POSITION**

When you need to perform another maneuver after a rein back, you don't want to finish the rein back with the horse's legs sprawled out behind him since this would make it difficult for you to organize the horse to perform the next maneuver. Diminish your rein back aids on the fifth step backward so that your horse isn't in the middle of a large step when you finish the rein back. This will put you in a better position to prepare for your 90-degree turn. Since it is a turn on the forehand to the left, the first step will be the left hind stepping over in front of the right hind. Therefore, ideally you want to finish the rein back with your horse's right hind leg slightly behind your horse's left hind leg, which will make crossover smooth. If you halt with the left hind leg next to or behind the right hind leg, your horse will need to take a step forward or backward to get into position or he might step on his right foot with his left, neither of which is polished.

PATTERN 100

A   Trot right diagonal

B   Canter left lead
    Counter-canter right circle

C   Canter circle to left

C   Flying change

D   Halt
    Rein back 4 steps
    Walk
    Join new lineup

Pattern Help

A Trot right diagonal. (See Pattern 59.)

B Canter left lead. (See Pattern 55.)

Counter-canter right circle. After you complete the counter-canter circle, you will canter straight ahead for a few strides on the left lead to cone C. (See Tip at right and Pattern 96.)

C Canter circle to left on the left lead. The first time you pass cone C, it will be to bend left and ride a circle to the left on the left lead. (See Pattern 51.)

C Flying change to right lead. The next time you pass cone C, you will perform a flying change left to right and canter straight ahead toward cone D. The change should occur when your shoulders pass cone C. (See Pattern 90.)

D Halt. (See Pattern 59.)

Rein back 4 steps. (See Pattern 58.)

Walk. (See Pattern 60.)

Join the new lineup.

TIP PREVENT FLYING CHANGE

Sometimes you will have to ride assertively to prevent your horse from performing a flying lead change. For example, in this pattern, when you canter left lead at cone B and then immediately turn into the right to begin the circle, your horse might very likely want, or think that you want him, to perform a flying lead change. It would be natural. Therefore, you must assure him that he is to remain on the left lead on the circle to the right. You do this by maintaining your left lead aids a little more strongly just as you begin the turn right. Be sure your right leg is behind the girth, your left leg at the girth and you have the horse slightly curled around your left leg and flexed to the left with your rein aids.

A Canter right lead

B Turn left counter-
   cantering

   Flying change

C Halt

   180-degree turn on the
   forehand left

   Canter right lead

B Halt

   Rein back 5 steps

   180-degree turn on the
   haunches right

   Trot through cone C

   Return to lineup

A

B

C

PATTERN HELP

A Canter right lead. (See Pattern 66.)

B Turn left counter-cantering. (See Patterns 68, 82, and 96.)

After corner, flying change to left lead.

Check. Be sure that your horse is cantering a 3-beat canter, his body is straight, and you feel contact with your horse through the reins.

Pre-change Positioning. With your horse cantering on the right lead, move your hands over to the right. You are shifting the horse's weight to his right side much like you do for a canter depart. At the same time, put your left leg on the horse to move him over to the right. When you are cantering on the right lead, your right seat bone is more forward than your left seat bone. Hold this pre-change position for 1 stride.

The Change. For the change, keep the horse straight and up on his right shoulder so that his left shoulder is "free" to change. Also, be sure you have contact to prevent a speedup during the change. You do this by maintaining contact with the right supporting rein.

Simultaneously, relax the pressure of your left leg that is holding the horse to the right (this "invites" the horse to the left) and move your left seat bone forward; apply your right leg behind the girth to ask for the change just as you would for a canter depart. (See Pattern 90.)

C Halt. (See Pattern 59.)

180-degree turn on the forehand left. (See Pattern 97.)

Canter right lead. (See Pattern 94.)

B Halt. (See Pattern 59.)

Rein back 5 steps. (See Tip below and Pattern 58.)

180-degree turn on the haunches right. (See Pattern 78.)

Trot through cone C. Since you will eventually be turning to the left, you should post on the right diagonal. (See Patterns 52 and 59.)

Return to the lineup.

TIP | THE TAIL END: PROTECTING YOUR HORSE'S TAIL

This pattern is a killer on long beautiful tails. Sliding stops and long rein backs are the biggest threat to a long tail and can make a horse reluctant to back. When the horse stops, his haunches drop, so the end of his tail is often laying on the dirt. When the horse starts backing, it is easy for him to step on the end of his tail and pull out large hunks all the way up to the dock. It doesn't take too many occurrences to result in a very thin tail. And when a horse steps on a large hunk of hair and yanks it out, it hurts. It could make him shy of backing in the future. Horses also can pull out large sections of tail when they are unloading from a trailer. That's why the tails of trailered horses are usually braided, wrapped, or bagged for loading, unloading, and traveling.

To protect your horse's tail, keep it trimmed so that the end is at the point of your horse's fetlock when the horse's tail is relaxed and flat on his anus (not raised). That way when your horse is working, it will be slightly above this point, which is a fairly safe level. A blunt cut tail (banged) is less wispy on the ends than a tapered tail so it tends to look thicker, and it's easier to keep trimmed regularly.

Appendix

HORSE SHOW CHECKLISTS

I suggest you develop a series of checklists that you can use each time you prepare for a show. You may wish to keep certain lists in your house, others in your tack room, and a master list in your truck or trailer. Refer to your checklists, but realize that they are not foolproof and it is possible that you might leave an important item at home. Have Plans B and C ready so that you don't fall apart if you arrive at the show and find you left something behind.

PAPERWORK CHECKLIST

- ❏ Original or photocopy of registration papers
- ❏ Coggins test certification
- ❏ Health exam certification
- ❏ Proof of ownership
- ❏ Amateur or Non-Pro card
- ❏ Association membership card
- ❏ Proof of age — Youth exhibitors
- ❏ Show bill
- ❏ Rule book
- ❏ Paper and pencils

FOR THE RIDER

- ❏ Coat or vest
- ❏ Pants
- ❏ Chaps
- ❏ Shirt
- ❏ Tie or pin
- ❏ Boots
- ❏ Spurs
- ❏ Gloves
- ❏ Hat, show type
- ❏ Hat, for sun protection
- ❏ Hair net
- ❏ Pins
- ❏ Comb
- ❏ Brush
- ❏ Safety pins
- ❏ Mirror
- ❏ Rain gear
- ❏ Rubber shoes/boots
- ❏ Nutritious snacks
- ❏ Water
- ❏ Folding chairs

HORSE CARE ITEMS

- ❏ Grain and feed tub
- ❏ Grain
- ❏ Hay net or bag
- ❏ Hay
- ❏ Water pail
- ❏ Water, if necessary
- ❏ Oil of wintergreen, apple juice, or powdered electrolyte drink (Gatorade), if your horse requires flavored drinking water when away from home
- ❏ Electrolyte paste or powder
- ❏ Manure fork and bucket or basket
- ❏ Barn broom
- ❏ Rake
- ❏ Bedding (shavings or straw)
- ❏ Barn lime
- ❏ Horse blanket and hood
- ❏ Sheet or fly net
- ❏ Fly repellent

TACK & TACK CARE

Tack

- ❏ Saddle
- ❏ Bridle
- ❏ Martingale
- ❏ Pad or blanket
- ❏ Girth or cinch
- ❏ Lead rope
- ❏ Protective boots
- ❏ Tack trunk
- ❏ Extra halter and lead rope

Tack Care

- ❏ Sponges
- ❏ Cloths
- ❏ Saddle soap
- ❏ Polish
- ❏ Small bucket

GROOMING KIT

- ❑ Hoof pick
- ❑ Rubber curry
- ❑ Dandy brush
- ❑ Body brush
- ❑ Rubber mitts
- ❑ Rub rags
- ❑ Sponge
- ❑ Sweat scraper
- ❑ Bucket
- ❑ Shampoo
- ❑ Hose
- ❑ Corn starch
- ❑ Baby oil
- ❑ Hoof sealer
- ❑ Hoof black
- ❑ Electric and battery-operated clippers
- ❑ Comb
- ❑ Hairbrush
- ❑ Yarn and needle for Hunter classes
- ❑ Rubber bands or tape
- ❑ Scissors
- ❑ Extra tail wrap

FIRST AID

- ❑ Iodine-based antiseptic solution
- ❑ Triple antibiotic ointment
- ❑ Nonstick gauze pads
- ❑ Self-conforming gauze rolls
- ❑ Stretch bandaging tape
- ❑ Elastic adhesive tape
- ❑ Scissors
- ❑ Cotton or disposable diaper
- ❑ Chemical ice pack
- ❑ Liniment
- ❑ Sunscreen

MISCELLANEOUS

- ❑ Plastic bags
- ❑ Extra cloths

TRAVELING

- ❑ Traveling blanket
- ❑ Shipping boots
- ❑ Tail wrap
- ❑ Halter and lead rope

Some Breed and Performance Organizations That Conduct Horsemanship and Equitation Classes

American Horse Shows Association (AHSA)
4047 Iron Works Parkway
Lexington, KY 40511
www.ahsa.org
Hunt Seat Equitation, Saddle Seat Equitation, Dressage Equitation, and Stock Seat Equitation for Arabian, Saddlebred, Morgans and other breeds

American Quarter Horse Association (AQHA)
P.O. Box 200
Amarillo, TX 79168-0001
www.aqha.com
Hunt Seat Equitation on the Flat and Western Horsemanship for Registered American Quarter Horses

American Paint Horse Association (APHA)
P.O. Box 961023
Fort Worth, TX 76161-0023
www.apha.com
Hunt Seat Equitation and Western Horsemanship (Equitation) for Registered American Paint Horses

Appaloosa Horse Club (APHC)
P.O. Box 8403
Moscow, ID 83843-0903
aphc@appaloosa.com
Hunt Seat Equitation, Western Equitation, and Saddle Seat Equitation for Registered Appaloosa Horses

Palomino Horse Breeders of America, Inc. (PHBA)
15253 E. Skelly Dr.
Tulsa, OK 74116-2637
Yellahrses@aol.com
Hunt Seat Equitation and Western Horsemanship for Registered Palomino horses

4-H Organizations
Contact your local agricultural extension agent to obtain a copy of your state 4-H rule book.
Western Horsemanship, Hunt Seat Equitation, Saddle Seat Equitation for all breeds of registered and unregistered horses of any breed

Index

Note: Page numbers in **boldface** indicate charts.

Other Storey Titles You Will Enjoy

Becoming an Effective Rider: Developing Your Mind and Body for Balance and Unity by Cherry Hill. Riders learn to evaluate their own skills, plan a work session, get maximum use out of lesson time, set goals and achieve them, and protect themselves from injury. 192 pages. Paperback. ISBN 0-88266-688-6.

From the Center of the Ring: An Inside View of Horse Competitions by Cherry Hill. The inside secrets of equestrian competition, including Western and English events, protocol, tack and clothing, grooming, and etiquette. 192 pages. Paperback. ISBN 0-88266-494-8.

Getting the Most from Riding Lessons by Mike Smith. A reassuring introduction to riding, this book helps novice riders maximize the lesson experience, providing information about safety, horse behavior, basic riding exercises, and preparing for that first show. 160 pages. Paperback. ISBN 1-58017-082-X.

Getting Your First Horse by Judith Dutson. This book answers hundreds of questions prospective horse owners have: What do I need to know to choose a horse? What will my horse need for housing, feed, exercise? How much will all this cost? Medical terms, handling techniques, and a compendium of breeds are included. 176 pages. Paperback. ISBN 1-58017-078-1.

Horse Handling & Grooming: A Step-by-Step Photographic Guide by Cherry Hill. This user-friendly guide to essential skills includes feeding, haltering, tying, grooming, clipping, bathing, braiding, and blanketing. The wealth of practical advice offered is thorough enough for beginners, yet useful for experienced riders improving or expanding their skills. 160 pages. Paperback. ISBN 0-88266-956-7.

Horse Health Care: A Step-by-Step Photographic Guide by Cherry Hill. Explains bandaging, giving shots, examining teeth, deworming, and preventive care. Exercising and cooling down, hoof care, and tending wounds are depicted, along with taking a horse's temperature, and determining pulse and respiration rates. 160 pages. Paperback. ISBN 0-88266-955-9.

Horse Sense: A Complete Guide to Horse Selection & Care by John J. Mettler Jr., D.V.M. Covers selecting, housing, fencing, and feeding a horse plus immunizations, dental care, and breeding. 160 pages. Paperback. ISBN 0-88266-545-6.

101 Arena Exercises: A Ringside Guide for Horse & Rider by Cherry Hill. Classic exercises and original patterns and drills are presented in a unique "read-and-ride" format. The book can be hung like a calendar or draped over the rail for easy reference. Exercises progress through skill levels for both English and Western Riders. 224 pages. Paperback. ISBN 0-88266-316-X.

Taking Up Riding as an Adult by Diana Delmar. For adults who dream of riding but believe this is a skill that must be mastered in childhood, this book offers step-by-step advice for achieving that dream. 160 pages. Paperback. ISBN 1-58017-081-1.

These and other Storey Books are available at your bookstore, farm store, garden center, or directly from Storey Books, Schoolhouse Road, Pownal, Vermont 05261, or by calling 1-800-441-5700. Visit our Web site at www.storey.com